# ACKNOWLEDGMENTS

This book was really written by the college students who generously shared with me their problems, solutions, and experience in order to help other students in a similar situation. Without them, there would not have been a college cookbook.

I would especially like to thank the following students whose recipes appear in this book: Gayle Adler, James Adler, Ann Alter, Jeffrey Travis Atwood, Deborah Bachtel, Peggy Barlett, Jodi Bernstein, Bill Blainey, Robert Blake, Paul C. Bongiorno, Valerie Borchardt, Patrick Bowe, Barbara Brennecke, Michael Brennecke, Patricia Brennecke, Gerald Britain, Beliz Brother, Denise Brown, Ellyn L. Brown, Anne Bruner, Janice Corcoran, Patty Courtright, Judith Cruise, Marilyn Dey, Lynn Eaton, Robin Eigerman, Lynn Eninger, Daniela von Estorff, Dick Farrell, Naomi Fifield, Adam Foster, Mark W. Gardner, Wendy Gardner, Elaine R. Giampietro, Esther Greene, Galen Gregory, Jeanine Hardison, Noralyn Harlow, June Harris, Lee Anne Hartley, Bruce Heinze, Sabrina Herzog, Ralph Howland, Bill Jackson, Kim Jackson, Peta Jackson, Lois B. Jacobs, M. R. Johnson, Danny Kaplan, Linda Veum Kindler, Susan Leclerc, Susannah Levine, David Lovejoy, Patty Lyman, Kyle MacAusland, Lynn MacAusland, Margaret A. Machulis, Peter Macky, Kent Madin, Sue Maxwell, Michael Nathan, Lawrence N. Neber, Jonathan Olom, Noralyn Olom, R. Wayne Parker, Ellen Paul, Creighton Peet, Ann Petranoff, Joanna H. Phinney, Carol Plotkin, Sandra Poffenbarger, Catherine M. Preus, Guy Rabut, Debbie Reading, Keith _____, Phyllis B. Rosenberg, Peg Rourke, Jo Ann Schoef, Nancy Schubert, Joan Shafran, Lisa Shattuck, Guerolan Smith, Shari Sobol, Mary Strong, James Swanzy, Tillie Taylor, Lesley Tegenborg, Dottie Thach, Ellen F. Thompson, Tim Thompson, Claudia Velletri, Gerry Vogt, Nancy Watson, Arthur Wells, Susan Welti, Sarah White, Debi Yaglinski, Liz Yoder.

In the case of duplicate recipes, I tended to credit the first student who sent it in. But I would like to list the colleges whose students took time out from their busy schedules to correspond with me and to fill out patiently and return my lengthy questionnaires, and those who sent in recipes but did not sign their names or do not have their recipes included in this edition: Barnard College, Bennington College, Boston College, Boston University, University of Bridgeport, University of California (Berkeley), University of California (Davis), University of California (Irvine), University of California (Los Angeles), University of California (Santa Barbara), University of Colorado, Columbia University, University of Connecticut, Cornell University, Curtis Institute of Music (Philadelphia), University of Delaware, University of Denver, Duke University, Georgetown University, George Washington University, Goddard College, Harvard University, Hobart College, Indiana University, Johns Hopkins University, Humboldt State University, University of Louisville, University of Maine, University of

Maryland, Massachusetts Institute of Technology, University of Miami, University of Michigan, Middlebury College, Mills College, University of Minnesota, Nasson College, New England Conservatory of Music, University of New Hampshire, University of New Mexico, New York University, University of North Carolina (Chapel Hill), University of Northern Colorado, Northwestern University, University of Oregon, Peabody Conservatory of Music (Baltimore), University of Pennsylvania, University of Pittsburgh, Prescott College, Rice University, Rutgers University, Smith College, School of the Museum of Fine Arts (Boston), Stanford University, Syracuse University, University of Texas, Texas Christian University, Tulane University, Union College (Schenectady), Upsala College (Wirths Campus), Vassar College, University of Vermont, University of Virginia, Wesleyan, Williams College, William Smith College, Yale University.

In addition, this book would never have gotten out of the kitchen without the help of Lynn Eaton and Barbara Ann Homan who tested so many of the recipes—often making a dish several times in order to work out the quantities and proportions when they were not given in the original recipe.

Finally, I would like to express my gratitude and appreciation to all the students throughout the country whose warm response, enthusiasm, advice, and suggestions made writing this book such a pleasure.

# CONTENTS

# INTRODUCTION

A recent study confirms what students and I have always known—the stereotype of the student as a fast food junkie living on a steady diet of french fries and Cokes bears no resemblance to the true picture. In fact, as the study revealed, many students are more knowledgeable about nutrition than their parents, and care enough about what they eat to take a deep and active interest in preparing their own meals. Fortunately, colleges have reluctantly faced these facts and many now provide student refrigerators, as well as kitchens on many dorm floors, with some even building new housing facilities designed for several students living together in apartments.

These recipes, compiled from the hundreds sent to me by students around the country, reflect the present student lifestyle—short of time and money but not of creativity, and more than open to new ideas. Free of traditional food prejudices, influenced by world travel, students today like and make for themselves food that is based on many cultures, ethnic groups, and unusual combinations. Mexican, Chinese, Indian, Hungarian, Spanish, South American, and French are only some of the cuisines that contribute the dishes they prepare routinely. They cherish their own recipes and will argue vehemently as to whether chili should be made with or without tomatoes, or what combination of foods makes the best paella. They read labels carefully and

have nothing but scorn for cottage cheese that contains "flavoring," or junk foods richer in additives than in nutrients. My own cupboard contents have changed drastically over the years since my sons did a bit of consciousness-raising on this subject, and I now know better than to buy anything that contains artificial coloring—at least, if I am aware of it. Students also know about the dangers of nitrates and nitrites, and their consumption of hot dogs and bacon has dropped accordingly.

With all of this they are not health food fanatics; they strike a remarkably happy balance. They do not blindly accept the merchandise in health food stores. By the time they complete their education, they have consumer awareness, a pleasure in their own domestic skills, and a respect for their bodies and what they fuel them with; I only hope they stick to their convictions.

I have very much enjoyed doing this book and working with students around the country. My only regret is that I have had to omit hundreds of fine recipes sent to me because there was simply not enough space for them all. I hope you like the ones I have included. Remember, I rely on the feedback I get from my readers to tell me where I have succeeded and where I have gone wrong. If you especially like a recipe and want more like it, let me know; if you don't like a recipe or have a suggestion for improving it, tell me about it. This is your book for your use, and I would like it to reflect your tastes and needs; I particularly would like it to include your favorite recipes so that—through the printed word—they can be shared with other students with the same problems and lifestyles.

In closing, I would like to thank you all for your warm reception of my first book which has made this new edition possible. I hope you like this new version as well as you did the first. If you have any questions or care to write me about your own way of doing things, I would very much like to hear from you.

*Geri Harrington*
*Merwin Lane*
*Wilton, Connecticut*

# EAT BETTER FOR LESS

In times of rising prices, shopping economically requires fast footwork because the rules change as fast as you learn them. However, there are still some things you can do to get the most for your food money.

If you are **doing your own cooking**, you have already taken the first, and most important, step in eating better for less. You can afford to eat steak at home for possibly less than you would pay for hamburger in a restaurant, and you know it's steak—not hamburger made from what might be a dubious cut of meat.

But to get the most value from your own cooking, you have to learn how to cook. Generally speaking, **the most expensive things are the easiest to cook**. Cheaper, equally delicious foods, take a little more skill. Learning to cook is a cumulative process; the more you know, the easier it is to learn more. Master the basics and you won't have any trouble with more complicated recipes. The important thing is to understand why you are doing things. Many people follow recipes blindly all their lives and couldn't improvise if survival depended on it. Don't cook like that. Learn how to make soup, stew, a casserole, etc., in a general sort of way and then you can improvise to suit your budget or what happens to be on hand.

**Next to eating out, the most expensive thing you can do is to use so-called "conven-ience" foods**. The more that's been done to a food, the more it costs and the less good it is for you. Frozen TV dinners are a perfect example. They are handy and if you eat two of them, you feel full. But a little planning will enable you to have home-made, easy-to-heat-up casseroles in your own re-frigerator, and they won't contain preservatives and all sorts of artificial "flavor enhancers" and other junk. If you buy frozen vegetables, don't get the ones with built-in sauces or seasonings. You pay a tremendous price for those extras, and you can add them yourself in a minute at little cost. Sauces are simple to make once you get over thinking you can't cook them, and mixed vegetables are no harder to fix from scratch than all of one kind. If you want an example of how much so-called convenience foods are costing you, compare the price of a can of cooked rice with the price of a box of rice and figure out your cost per serving. To save that money all you have to do is wait for the rice to cook. You don't even have to watch it or pay any attention to it while it's cooking.

Another way to save money is to **buy the week's specials**. If you don't like what one market is featuring, maybe another nearby has something else. It's possible to save as much as forty to fifty cents a pound on meat if you buy it on "special." It also adds interest to eating. I didn't buy lamb for six weeks this summer because it never went on "special." When it finally did, I bought a leg and we enjoyed it extra-specially because we hadn't had it for so long and thought of it as a real treat.

There is one thing to beware of in buying bargains. The supermarkets know you are looking for specials, so they try to make regularly priced items look special by displaying them as if they were. **If an item is featured, make sure it is actually priced lower than usual**. This means knowing your prices, but if you shop regularly and don't have much money to spend, you will automatically remember what most of your purchases cost. Take a minute to think back to what you paid for it last time and don't touch if it is not a bargain no matter how large a stack of cans they may have pyramided to entice you. Of course, you can't buy *just* bargains, but even staples like sugar and hamburger go up and down in price. So do the best you can to buy when things are temporarily lower. Just keep in mind that not all featured items are bargains.

**Don't buy dented cans even if they are a bargain**. Your doctor bills may more than make up the difference in price.

**Don't buy vegetables that look downright old or you will be cheating yourself of the vitamins and minerals you should be getting**. But **late Saturday afternoon may offer markdowns** in fresh produce which won't keep over the weekend. *Slightly* tired lettuce, etc., may still be good to eat. *Slightly* browned mushrooms are often a very good buy.

Whenever possible, **buy in a market where you can select your own fruits and vegetables** instead of buying them bagged or in a tray. Some supermarkets package lemons with a few fresh and a few on the old side. If you pick them out individually, you pick out only top quality. This is true of grapes, cherries, etc., too. But if you do buy oranges by the bag (sometimes the cheapest way), look at all the oranges through the plastic to make sure none are spoiled. You can return the spoiled ones and get good fruit in exchange, but that takes a lot of time. If a head of lettuce or escarole has been trimmed so that the dark outer leaves are gone and you can see whitish yellow on the bottom of the outside leaves, that head has been trimmed down because it's old. Not only are you losing the outer dark green leaves which contain the most nutrients, you are buying older greens they had to trim to sell. Let someone else buy them.

**Always smell boxes of strawberries before you buy them**. If they are fragrant and the berries look plump and perfect through all the slits in the sides of the box, they are good berries. If they have a slightly rotten smell, or no smell at all, or have a lot of mashed berries showing on the sides, get something else that day. If even one berry is moldy, pass up that box.

**Buy fruits and vegetables in season**. When asparagus first comes on the market, it is a luxury. Two weeks later, you can afford to make a meal of it. The same is true with fruits. So have a little patience. Things in season will not only be cheaper, they will taste better. The pleasure of anticipation will add to your enjoyment when you finally eat them.

If you eat much meat, it is the most expensive part of your food budget, so it's worth learning to buy it wisely. **Get to know what a good**

**piece of meat looks like**. Meat that looks dried out or off-color can easily be recognized even by someone inexperienced. Usually in a supermarket fresh packages of meat and old packages are in the case at the same time. Look around and see if you can spot one of each. The fresh meat will generally look much more attractive than the old meat; once you have seen the difference, you won't be stuck with old meat. Sometimes you can decipher the store's dating code by watching the clerk replenish the cases. Notice the packages she is putting down and compare them with the ones already in the case. You will soon figure out the code. It's never very complicated.

If you're on a tight budget, **don't feel there's nothing between sirloin steak and hamburger**. There are bone-in chuck steaks which cost about the same price as hamburger and make great broiled steaks. Get the cut nearest the rib rather than toward the neck. If it seems tough the first time you try it, marinate it next time and you will be very happy with it. It also provides the basis for lots of dishes—like pepper steak which taste great, are a real change from broiled meat, and stretch a pound of meat to feed eight people (with rice, vegetables, etc.) A friendly butcher will answer questions honestly and teach you about the various cuts of meat. Or get a book from the library and learn one cut at a time. A couple of weeks of this will save you a small fortune the rest of your life and make eating much more interesting. Who would want to live on just broiled steak, broiled chicken, and hamburgers, even if they could afford it?

**Whenever possible, shop in a good part of town**. Surveys have shown that inner-city mar-

kets actually charge more. Another advantage of shopping in a good section is that the overall quality of the food will be more closely controlled. Customers are fussier and won't hesitate to make a commotion if something is unsatisfactory. Also, cheaper cuts of meat are not as much in demand, so they are usually priced somewhat lower than in poor neighborhoods where everyone wants them. Supermarkets usually charge less than independent butchers for things like kidneys, brains, chicken livers, etc., so keep an eye out for them and buy them when you see them (rather than make up your mind ahead of time that that is what you are going to have for dinner).

When it comes to brands of canned goods, **often the store's own brands are your best buy**. They may even be national brands packed under the store's label, in which case, you get a bargain by paying less for exactly the same quality. Stores usually have two grades which they pack under two different names. Check them out by buying one of each and see what you're paying for. Sometimes it is worth it, sometimes it is not. I find that canned tomatoes vary a great deal in flavor and usually it's worth buying the market's own top grade. In frozen foods, you have the same choice between name brands and store brands. Only experimenting will tell you about quality. However, sometimes the same frozen foods will vary from store to store of the same chain. This is because so much depends on how the food is kept; not all store managers are equally careful. Find a clean, well-managed supermarket and you will have more confidence in what you buy there.

You will save the most on your food bill by **joining or forming a cooperative**. Many groups of students on the West Coast have done this. They buy direct from the farmers at wholesale prices. If you cannot do this, sometimes you can make an arrangement with an independent grocer to give you special prices on the items you use in quantity and could buy by the case. Case lot prices make sense if you can buy for a large enough group and have the room to store that quantity. However, this is not feasible for most students.

**Learn to read labels**. They don't give you nearly as much information as they should, but at least learn what you can from them. The first thing to know is that labels are required by law to **have their contents listed in order of quantity**; the ingredient there is most of is listed first, etc. A can that lists water as its first ingredient contains more water than anything else. If it lists "water, cereal, kidney beans, meat" in that order, you can figure you're not getting much meat. This can be a real giveaway as to the contents of a can, so always take the trouble to read it. Sometimes if you are wondering which of two brands to buy, the cheaper brand will show by its list of contents that it isn't as good a buy as the more expensive one. Anyway, always look.

The United States Government specifies standards for certain terms and this is protection for you **if you know what the terms mean**. "Fruit juice" contains all real fruit juice, whereas "nectar" or "punch" may be mostly water and sugar with artificial coloring. "Luncheon meat" has more meat than "meat loaf," which is allowed to have more cereal as filler. Meat spreads may be delicious but they contain only about half meat. Make your own very cheaply with a blender and some

spices, and know what you're eating. Natural cheese is hard to find but it's a much better buy than processed cheese, which contains much more moisture, less milk fat, and is sometimes loaded with chemicals. "Cheese food" may be only 20 percent cheese and 80 percent filler, vegetable gum, etc. Make your own chili. You can load it with beans and still get more meat than you would in a can.

Unfortunately, some foods—like ice cream and mayonnaise—don't have to tell you what is in them. They can have artificial coloring, artificial flavoring, or preservatives galore without a word about it on the package. Fortunately, some brands are now making a point of their purity, so **try to buy the brand that seems to care the most about the consumer**. Watch out when you buy yogurt. If the package lists anything unfamiliar as an ingredient, why buy it? Everything needed to make yogurt properly is something you would recognize as a normal ingredient. You will pay more for the real thing but anything else isn't worth eating. Same way with cottage cheese—it should be very fresh and not contain preservatives to extend its "shelf life" for three months or more. I'll never understand why anyone would need to add "artificial flavoring" to properly made cottage cheese. I won't buy cottage cheese if it has anything extra in it.

You would think you would be safe from additives when you buy raw meat. Unfortunately, this is not always true. For instance, smoked hams for baking are often labeled "water added." This means, aside from anything else, that **you are paying baked ham prices for water—sometimes quite a lot of water**. The meat will seem cheap if you just compare the price per pound to other hams, but it may be more expensive compared to what you are getting; it won't taste as good either. For the same reason, don't buy frozen turkeys with "butter" or any other fat added. You're paying extra for something you don't need. A good turkey is the easiest thing in the world to cook; it doesn't have to be doctored up for you.

It is usually considered good practice to buy the largest size package you have room to store. But larger packages are *not always* cheaper than the smaller ones. In fact, sometimes you pay proportionately more for the larger package. **So check before you buy**. For some reason this happens most often with detergents and things like that. It never seems to happen with tea, sugar, etc. However, packaging does make a difference in cost. Spices often come in both plain and fancy packages with a big difference in price for the same contents. Sugar, for instance, will usually be more cheaply packed in a bag than in a box. In one store the boxed sugar was exactly double the price of the identical sugar in the bag.

**How you intend using food should be a consideration** in buying it. Solid pack tuna may be desirable for a fancy salad plate, but chunk tuna would save time and money when making a casserole or a sandwich filling. Sliced canned peaches are a better buy than peach halves because they contain more fruit and less syrup. Don't buy a fancy pack unless you have a reason.

**Snacks can be a waste of time, money, and nutrition** if you eat what is commonly sold as snacks. Fruit and raw vegetables, nuts and seeds, natural juices, etc. make the best and most inexpensive snacks. When preparing vegetables for cooking (carrots, etc.), take an extra minute to make a few carrot sticks, keep out a few flowerets of cauliflower, etc., and use for snacks or in tomorrow's salad. Potato chips and all other deep-fat fried nibbles don't do a thing for you. I notice that most of you said you won't have a thing to do with them. Of course, once in a while, you may eat something thoroughly useless just for fun. But at least know what you're paying a pound for it. You might prefer lobster instead!

Some of you buy in health food stores in an effort to get better food, **but don't buy trustingly in them just because they sell "health foods."** Many of the same items they carry can be found at a more reasonable price in the supermarket; and you can't always be sure vegetables are organic unless you have grown them yourself. So while health food stores may be fun to shop in and sometimes have better products, shop there just as carefully as you would anywhere else.

If this makes shopping sound like a chore, it is. But it is fun, too. When you realize how much you can save by buying food knowledgeably and how well you can eat for much less than you thought, it's certainly worth it. Also, it's only hard in the beginning. After a while, it gets to be second nature and doesn't take much longer than just stuffing the shopping cart heedlessly.

**The best pots and pans you can buy are your best buy**. Good, heavy, well-made pots will last longer and cook more evenly. If you have trouble with everything sticking or burning, maybe your pots are too thin. Start out with just a few, but get good ones.

**Take proper care of your equipment**. Don't take a pot off the stove and put it in the sink, and don't put cold water in it when it's very hot. Give it a few minutes to cool, then fill with hot water and detergent and let it soak while you eat.

**Cast iron pots should never be really washed**. Just wipe clean with paper toweling. But be sure to follow manufacturer's directions for "seasoning" before using.

**Never scour stainless steel**. The scouring pad will make thousands of tiny scratches and the next time you cook, your food will stick.

For some reason students seem to gravitate toward enamel pots. They seem cheap—but if they are, don't buy them. A good enamel pot is very expensive. The cheap ones are either not real enamel or have a very thin layer of enamel and will chip and burn and not last at all. They also won't cook properly. If all you're going to do is boil water, they're easy to clean. But anything else you use them for may give you trouble unless you have very good quality.

# COMING TO TERMS

Cooking terms are a shortcut both in writing and in following recipes. For instance, if a recipe says "cream butter," you can read it faster and follow it more quickly if you know what "cream" means. If you don't know the meaning of a term, look it up the first couple of times. After that you will know just what to do. These are terms you asked for definitions of, or which you said you had trouble with when you were first learning to cook.

**BAKE.** To cook in an oven or similar enclosed space by dry heat. Obviously, a clambake is not cooked in a conventional oven, but is created by the sand, rocks, etc. Also there are devices which you can use on a top burner to bake small things like potatoes and muffins. These are sold in hardware stores and are helpful if all the equipment you have is a two-burner hot plate and you are crazy about baked potatoes.

**BARBECUE.** Anything cooked under a broiler with a barbecue sauce brushed on is said to be barbecued. Originally it was only applied to food cooked slowly over a turning spit or on a grill over charcoal. It's not very important as a description of a method of cooking but it's colorful in describing your dish. Barbecued spareribs sound much tastier somehow than broiled spareribs.

**BASTE.** To moisten food while cooking. Spooning pan juices over a roasting turkey is basting.

So is brushing on barbecue sauce while cooking spareribs. The idea is simply to keep the outside of whatever you are cooking from drying out. It also adds the flavor of your basting liquid and usually helps in browning the food. If you use plastic cooking bags, they are supposed to do the basting for you.

**BATTER.** You won't need to know about this unless you make pancakes or waffles from scratch, or certain fried foods. Batter is flour plus a liquid like milk or water, sometimes eggs, too, mixed all together to a consistency which can be poured or dropped from a spoon.

**BEAT.** You can beat with a spoon, fork, wire whisk, etc. What you are trying to do is add air to a mixture and get all the ingredients evenly mixed. Use rapid motions and get into all parts of the bowl, going down toward the bottom and lifting up to the top each time with a circular motion.

**BLANCH.** The confusion a lot of you find in this term is because it applies to three different things:
1. Mostly it means to cook something in boiling water for a very short time, not enough to cook it through but merely to soften it a little. In making stuffed cabbage, you blanch the cabbage leaves to soften them so they will bend without breaking when you roll them around the filling.

2. It also means the trick of dipping fruits and some vegetables in boiling water so you can peel them easily. If you need to peel tomatoes, for example, dip them in boiling water; the skin will come off easily, leaving a nice, neat peeled tomato. If it doesn't, pop it back into the boiling water and leave a minute longer.

3. The third meaning is almost the same, only you dip shelled nuts into boiling water to get the outer skin off.

It's no use trying to tell you how long to keep anything in boiling water (obviously cabbage leaves will take longer to "blanch" than tomatoes) but trial and error works fine. You won't spoil anything if you leave it in the water a little too long. Just don't throw out the boiling water until you are sure you are finished with it.

**BLEND.** To mix two or more ingredients together so that they are evenly distributed throughout the mixture. Sometimes you do this by just stirring, sometimes by beating or folding. It all depends on what is being combined.

**BOIL.** This term is simple but not very accurate. You need to know the difference between a racing boil, slow boil, and simmer.

*Racing boil.* Boiling over high heat so water is bubbling as fast as it can. This is important when cooking spaghetti or adding something to the water which should not stop the water boiling. It is very bad for cooking meat. As one student said in a recipe for stew:

> *Meat fast boiled*
> *Is meat half spoiled.*

*Slow boil.* Bubbles break the surface in a regular sort of pattern and look like what you think of as boiling. A slow boil does not churn the food around madly. Most vegetables should be boiled this way—steadily, but not frantically.

*Simmer.* The slowest boil of all. It means the bubbles rise and break just under the surface so that the water continually ripples. It is the only way to cook something long and slowly so as to bring out the most flavor. Stews, casseroles, and all other long-cooking dishes, whether top-of-the-stove or oven-cooked dishes, should be cooked this way. Don't cook it with a lower heat than this—it should never *stop* simmering—but not higher either. You will have to keep an eye on it in the beginning to be sure it is going to keep simmering, but then you can forget about it until it is done.

**BRAISE.** Even experienced cooks seem to find this a confusing term. I think that is because it is really two steps:

1. Brown the food in a small amount of cooking oil.
2. Cook slowly (simmer) in a small amount of liquid in a flat pan with a tight cover.

You first brown your meat on all sides, then add some liquid (soy sauce, wine, etc.), cover, and continue cooking until tender. This is great for the inexpensive but flavorful cuts of meat which are too tough for broiling or sautéing. The trick is to use only a small amount of liquid. If you use too much you will boil, not braise. Check every so often and add a little more liquid (even water), if necessary. Some things, like tomatoes or zucchini, are watery and add to the liquid you have put in the pan, so until you are experienced, start out with a minimum and increase it when you have simmered the dish for twenty minutes or so. You want to end up with enough liquid for a couple of spoonsful of gravy or sauce. You may remove the cooked food a few minutes before serving, keep it hot, and thicken the liquid in the pan with flour or cornstarch.

**BREAD.** To coat with cracker or bread crumbs. Sometimes the food is dipped in milk or a beaten egg first.

**BROIL.** To cook under the broiler unit in your oven or over a fire directly (not in a frying pan). If you cook in a frying pan without oil (or just enough oil to keep the food from sticking), it is called "pan broil" and has a similar effect in terms of taste. *Grill* is the same as *broil*.

**BUTTER.** To rub a pan or grill with butter or oil so food will not stick to it; it will be easier to clean. Good to do with baking dishes when making macaroni casseroles, etc. An easy way to do it is to put the butter or oil in the pan and rub it around with a piece of wax paper.

**CHOP.** Cutting things up has an effect on how long you have to cook them. So while chopping is a general term for cutting things into pieces, there are more specific terms which tell you how large the pieces are supposed to be.

*Mince.* To chop food as finely as possible, short of grinding. Usually done with garlic, onion, etc. when you want it to vanish into the sauce.

*Dice.* Pieces less than ½" square but not smaller than ¼".

*Cube.* Pieces ½" to 1" square.

*Chunks.* Large cubes, about 1½" to 2" square.

Most recipes will specify as above; some will actually say "cut meat in ¾" cubes." With vegetables, the terms are usually more general because size isn't as crucial (unless they are shredded or grated).

**CLARIFY.** Another term with more than one meaning:

*To clarify stock.* Add egg white, egg shells, or raw hamburger and simmer uncovered for 15-20 minutes. Then strain. This will give you a clear broth.

*To clarify butter.* Melt and heat until foamy. Spoon off the foam and carefully pour the clear butter into a container, being careful not to include the white solids in the bottom. The reason for this is that clarified butter is butter without the milk solids. It can be heated to a much higher temperature without burning and is, therefore, better for sautéing than regular butter. I keep a small cup of it in the refrigerator to use whenever I want to fry in butter. It keeps almost indefinitely.

**CREAM.** To soften butter or shortening by pressing it against the side of a bowl, preferably with a wooden spoon, until it is soft and smooth. Sometimes the butter is worked with sugar, as in making a cake. Sometimes it's just handy for making butter soft enough to spread on sandwiches without tearing the bread.

**CRISP.** Another two-meaning word:
1. When applied to raw vegetables, it means to make crisp by soaking briefly in ice water and refrigerating—like carrot strips, celery, etc.
2. When applied to cooking vegetables, it means to get a crisp outer shell on food by heating it

in the oven or under the broiler.

Which only proves that you have to use common sense when following a recipe or you will end up with a salad made of oven-fried carrots.

CUT. This is tricky because it sounds obvious:
1. To separate food into pieces by using scissors or knife.

But the most important meaning is:
2. To combine butter or shortening with dry ingredients by working them with two knives or a pastry blender. The action is basically a cutting action but the purpose is to mix the ingredients evenly and finely. Since, because of the nature of the things you are trying to combine you can't just stir them, you keep cutting down through the whole mixture until it looks homogeneous. This is important in making dough and there is no shortcut.

DEGLAZE. A lovely term, but all it means is getting off the pieces that are stuck on the bottom of a frying pan by adding water or wine or whatever liquid the recipe calls for, and simmering it while you loosen the burned-on bits with a wooden spoon. It takes about a minute to do, is the easiest way to clean a stuck-on pan, and also adds an incredible amount of flavor to your sauce or gravy.

DEGREASE. This is easy, too. It means to remove fat from the surface of liquids. There are lots of ways to do it. The best way is to cool the dish until the fat solidifies; it will all be on top and you can just pick it off. Or you can drop in a couple of ice cubes. The fat will congeal on them if you remove them immediately. Or brush a lettuce leaf across the surface; the fat will adhere to it.

You can spoon it off. Since the fat always floats on top of the liquid, you can remove the fat by just skimming the surface. This takes a little time and patience but, like the first method, it saves the fat for later use, if desired.

If you don't have time to cool the liquid, I find the spooning method works best, but not everyone does. Sometimes it's more efficient to pour the fat into a custard cup or bowl. You will get some of the broth with it but the fat will be in a thicker layer on top and easier to remove.

DEVIL. To mix something—for example, hard-boiled egg yolks—with mustard or some other hot seasoning. Very tasty and quick. Sprinkle with a dash of paprika and you have a company dish.

DOT. To put small dabs of butter here and there over the top of food before baking or broiling it. Usually the recipe will tell you about how much butter to start with, but common sense is a good guide. As the dish gets hot, see if there is melted butter all over it; if not, add a few more "dots."

DREDGE. About the same as "bread" except it is usually applied to coating something with flour. Easy to do if you put the flour in a plastic bag and put the pieces of meat in the bag and shake.

DRIPPINGS. Just what it sounds like. The fat and juice that drip from meat when it is cooking. Save it for gravies, soups, casseroles, or sauces, if desired. Put it in a jar in the refrigerator and label with tape so you know what kind of meat it came from (like "bacon drippings," "roast beef drippings").

**DUST.** To sprinkle flour, sugar, or any appropriate ingredient lightly over the surface of the food.

**EGGS, BEATEN.** Sometimes recipes will call for eggs beaten in various ways. It is usually important to beat them according to these instructions, so here are the terms:

*Lightly beaten.* Beat just enough to blend the yolks and whites.

*Well beaten.* As you continue from the lightly beaten stage, the eggs will become frothy and full of air.

*Egg whites, very stiff.* Separate the whites from the yolks. A simple way to do this is to break the egg in half over the edge of a custard cup, carefully so that you don't break the yolk. *Whites will not beat if there is even a drop of yolk in them.* Then pass the yolk back and forth from shell half to shell half over the cup, letting the white drip down into the cup. Some students do it by cradling the egg yolk in their hands and letting the white drip down between their fingers, but this is tricky.

Let the whites warm to room temperature and beat with a fork, whisk, or eggbeater until they stand up in peaks. The points of the peaks should not droop when the beater is removed. The surface of the whipped whites should not look too dry. Use beaten egg whites right away or they will liquefy and you will have to start all over again with new egg whites.

*Yolks, well beaten.* Separate from the whites as directed above. Then beat until they are thick in consistency and lemon-colored.

**FOLD.** A much gentler mixing action than any other. A way of combining ingredients when one of them is fragile, like beaten egg whites. If you combine them simply by stirring, the whole mixture will collapse; instead add whatever you are adding by putting the ingredient to be mixed into the egg white (or whipped cream, etc.) on top and then, gently, with a spoon or whip, cutting down and over so that the whole mixture is "folded" over and over until it is well mixed.

**FRY.** To cook in oil or butter in a pan on top of the stove. If you use no oil or very little, you are "grilling" or "pan-broiling." If you use a little oil, you are "sautéing." If you use a lot in a deep pan, you are "deep-fat frying" or "French frying."

The important thing about all frying methods is to get the oil hot enough so that the food will cook quickly, forming a crisp outer crust and absorbing as little oil as possible. Sometimes a recipe, for cooking in a wok, for instance, will tell you to get the oil "smoking hot." Usually this is too hot, but do it if the recipe says to and you have a good ventilator fan.

If you are cooking with butter, it is hot enough when the foam begins to subside. After that it will brown and then burn and you usually do not want this to happen until after you have your food in and cooking.

With an aluminum pan, heat the pan before putting in the butter or oil. With copper-clad pans, you must put the butter or oil in the cold pan; it damages the pan to heat it empty.

When pan broiling, keep pouring off any excess fat or the food will be greasy. In this sense, bacon is pan-broiled rather than pan-fried.

**GRATIN or GRATINÉED.** A term that looks good on menus or sounds elegant if someone wants to know what's for dinner. It means you covered the cooked food (leftovers, etc.) with a sauce, sprinkled grated cheese or buttered crumbs on top, and dotted the whole thing with butter before putting it in the oven to heat up. Sometimes if it hasn't browned enough in the oven heat, you stick it under the broiler for a minute to get nice and brown. It's an easy, inexpensive way to use up almost anything; if you do it a day or two after cooking the original ingredients, no one will think of it as leftovers gussied up.

**GRATE.** To cut food up into particles on a grater. There are various kinds. A good, efficient, inexpensive one that can be found in variety and hardware stores is four-sided, open at top and bottom, grates in varying degrees of fineness (depending on which side you use), and is a breeze to clean. The food drops down inside and is handy to push off the cutting board into the pot or salad bowl or measuring cup.

**GRILL.** *see* "Broil."

**GRIND.** To crush into very small particles or powder with a mortar and pestle or whatever you have that will do the job. Also, to grind meat, like hamburger, etc.

**JULIENNE.** To cut into thin strips, like matchsticks. This is used especially for potatoes and carrots, which are sufficiently hard to cut small and straight without making a mess. The carrots are good raw and the potatoes French-fried.

**KNEAD.** To make dough elastic by pressing into it with the heel of your hand until it is stretched and smooth. You have to keep lifting it up, folding it over, and pressing down. It's essential to most breadmaking and is a curiously satisfying feeling, like working with clay.

**LEAVENING.** Something which expands, aerates, and raises other ingredients, like yeast, baking powder, etc. in dough.

**LYONNAISE.** Another fancy term—it means you have added chopped onions to a dish. "Potatoes Lyonnaise," for instance.

**MARINATE.** To let food soak in a seasoned oil and acid (vinegar, lemon juice, etc.) mixture (called a "marinade"), usually three hours to overnight. It seasons and tenderizes and is good for tough cuts of meat which you want to broil (as in shish kebab). It is fun to use in unexpected ways—like marinating beef overnight before roasting. It means you can use the same cut of meat all week (if it is very cheap that week) and vary the seasonings to create completely different dishes. For instance, *Brazilian Beef Casserole* and *Chinese Pepper Ground Steak* vary mostly in the seasoning (coffee instead of soy sauce). It works with vegetables, too.

**MINCE.** *see* "Chop."

**PARE.** To cut off (with a knife or vegetable parer) any outside covering, like peeling a potato.

**POACH.** To cook food in gently boiling (simmering) liquid. Generally used for foods that would break up under rougher treatment (fish, eggs, etc.). Sometimes you have to wrap it in parchment or cheesecloth to keep it whole.

**PREHEAT.** To heat oven, broiler, etc. to cooking

temperature before putting in the food to be cooked. Very important. Take it for granted that you should do it unless the recipes specify a cold oven.

**PUNCH DOWN.** A term you need to know for baking. Actually punch the dough with your fist, flattening it out in that spot. This allows the gas that has been formed by yeast to escape and allows a fresh supply of oxygen to reach the yeast. Do it evenly and throughout the mass of dough.

**PUREE.** To mash into a baby-food-like consistency. A blender is good for this or you can press the soft food through a sieve. Most vegetables have to be cooked before they can be pureed.

**REDUCE.** A kind of cooking shorthand. You "reduce" the amount of liquid by boiling it down. For instance, one cup boiled down ("reduced") to three tablespoons. Most reducing can be done at a pretty fast boil. If you overdo it and come out with less than you are supposed to, just add the amount of hot water necessary to make up the right amount of liquid. You usually do it to concentrate the flavor.

**RENDER.** To melt fat into liquid. Use very low heat and take out the solids when you have as much fat as you need or have patience to wait for.

**RISE.** Another baking term. To let dough that has yeast in it rise in a warm place—usually to double its bulk, but follow the recipe.

**ROAST.** *See* "Bake." Most cookbooks will tell you not to add water to a roasting pan. I always

do because otherwise the fat burns on the bottom of the pan (unless you are cooking something with a lot of fat, like ham, in which case the fat gets too hot and smokes). A little water keeps the fat from burning or smoking and helps make juice or gravy. Don't add much, just enough to cover the bottom of the pan about ½". If it cooks off, add a little more.

There are also two schools of thought about roasting temperatures. One says start the roast at a high temperature to brown and seal the surface, and then reduce the heat for the rest of the cooking time. The other sets the oven at the second temperature to start with and cooks it a little longer. There are two advantages to the second method: you don't have to be around to turn the oven down after the first 15 minutes; the roast doesn't shrink so much, so you get more meat for your money. I much prefer this method. The meat browns beautifully either way.

**SAUTE.** *see* "Fry."

**SCALD.** A multiple-meaning term like so many others:
1. To heat to just below the boiling point. Very important with milk to avoid that "boiled" taste most people dislike. With milk, heat until tiny bubbles form around the edge of the pot and then take it quickly off. It must be watched while heating because it happens all of a sudden.
2. To dip in boiling water (*see* "Blanch").

**SCALLOP.** This is a term that is practically a recipe because it tells you to arrange food in layers in a casserole, pour sauce over it, sprinkle with a little flour, bread or cracker crumbs, dot with butter, and bake. An easy, tasty way to combine leftovers with a fresh vegetable and make a good dish—like cooked ham and sliced raw potatoes and onions.

**SHRED.** To tear, cut, or grate into long, flat, narrow pieces with a knife, grater, or shredder. Shredded things cook faster than chopped because they are thinner, so it is a good way to treat suitable vegetables. Just shred them, toss lightly in a skillet with hot butter or olive oil, season, and serve. (See recipe for *Shredded Zucchini*.)

**SIMMER.** *see* "Boil."

**SKIM.** To remove the top surface, like the fat on chicken soup, the foam on clarified butter, or cream on raw milk.

**STEEP.** To extract the flavor by soaking in a liquid. What you do when you make tea.

**STEW.** To cook in simmering liquid until tender. Do not ever let a stew boil faster than a simmer or you will lose flavor and tenderness.

**STOCK.** The liquid in which anything has been cooked, for example, meat, vegetables, etc. Usually to make a really good stock you start the food in cold water. This extracts most of the nutrients and flavor. Strain when done and throw away the solids. If it happens to be meat, it is too costly to waste, so you eat it, but the taste usually needs a boost, like horseradish sauce for boiled beef. To make soup, add whatever meat and vegetables you wish and cook in the hot stock until tender.

**TOAST.** To crisp and brown by means of dry heat (usually on a flat pan in the oven). If you want to toast bread without an oven or toaster, put a fork through one end and hold over your hot plate, turning as necessary.

**TOSS.** To mix by lifting the bottom ingredients to the top so that the top falls to the bottom. Should be done with two large spoons or a large spoon and a large fork, without bruising the ingredients as in tossed salad.

**WHIP.** To beat ingredients that will incorporate air in such a way as to get fluffy—like heavy cream, egg whites. Heavy cream should be cold—egg whites at room temperature. Beat as fast as possible. If you beat whipped cream too stiff, you will end up with butter.

# COOKING HINTS

### THINGS NO ONE EVER THINKS TO TELL YOU

*No recipe ever starts at the beginning.* It assumes familiarity with certain basic terms, ingredients, and cooking methods. The novice cook has to resign himself or herself to some mistakes; even a very experienced cook will occasionally read a new recipe with a certain degree of puzzlement. There is also the hazard of recipes that have had some essential step or ingredient inadvertently left out. Even *The New York Times* has had to publish corrections and additions to a previous day's recipes. If you find a recipe in a cookbook that doesn't seem to work for you, don't struggle with it too hard. Maybe it wouldn't work for anyone. Of course, I hope that doesn't apply to any of the recipes in this book.

*Most recipes do not have to be followed exactly*, as you will realize when you watch someone at the table add half a shaker of salt to a dish you carefully made with exactly the ½ teaspoon the recipe called for. The recipes that do have to be followed exactly are those for baking bread, cake, etc., or dishes that you want to jell.

*Almost any recipe is a jumping-off place for a dozen variations.* You can substitute other vegetables, meats, or seasonings. But not indiscriminately, so start out easy. Sometimes just adding or leaving out something as simple as a can of tomatoes will make a completely different dish. To be on the safe side, taste any new dish before you serve it. If it seems lacking, think about combinations you have liked in other dishes. Sometimes all it needs is a flavor boost, and you can save the day by adding a bouillon cube.

When you first start cooking, *keep ingredients simple and as few as possible.* Too many things tend to cancel out one another.

*Notice how different methods of cooking affect the taste and texture of food.* Broiled chicken and boiled chicken, for instance, are very different. Once you have the difference clearly in mind, you will know instinctively that boiled chicken will make a better salad. This is a great help when you start to improvise.

*Seasoning is a personal matter.* In testing one of the recipes in this book, I fed the result to four people. One said it needed salt but was fine otherwise; one wanted much more chili; another a little less. I thought it needed a little garlic, but then I always do unless it's chocolate fudge. The point is that you have to season lightly until you find out how you want it to taste. Use less rather than more of a seasoning and you won't go wrong. Too little won't make a dish inedible; too much will.

### TO MEASURE ACCURATELY AND EASILY

*Dry ingredients.* Use a metal or plastic measuring cup that fills to the top. Fill cup on level surface and smooth off excess with a knife so top is level. For less than a cup, fill to the correct mark and shake slightly to level.

*Liquid ingredients.* Use glass measuring cup that does not fill to the top. Put on flat surface and bend down so your eye is level with the mark. A tall person who doesn't bend down can end up with an eighth of a cup less than he or she means to.

*Solid ingredients.* Fill measuring cup with amount of water equal to the amount of the solid ingredient your recipe calls for. Then add your ingredient until the water measures twice the amount. For example, to measure ½ cup butter: put in ½ cup water; add butter until water reaches 1 cup mark.

Some people have trouble with this, but I have never found a better way, and would love to know if anyone else has. Sometimes the butter is marked on the package in various measures, or you know that so many ounces of something equals so many cups, etc., but sooner or later you are going to have to measure something this way, so you might as well know how.

## ALTITUDE ADJUSTMENTS

If you go to the University of Denver or cook in a similarly high altitude, you will have to make certain adjustments in your recipes. Water boils at 212° F at sea level, at 194° F at 10,000 feet, so you have to cook stews, soups, or even eggs longer at higher altitudes because boiling water is not as hot as at sea level. There are books with special recipes for high-altitude cooking, or you can experiment a little. Your common sense will help you to figure out things like needing more water if you are boiling something longer.

## TIMING A RECIPE TO MAKE EVERYTHING COME OUT AT THE SAME TIME

In figuring out how long a recipe takes to make, allow plenty of time for preparation. A recipe that says "bake diced carrots and sliced potatoes for ½ hour" sounds clear enough. But you have to get the carrots and potatoes out of the vegetable bin, wash them, peel them, and dice them. Then you have to grease the casserole, heat the oven if you forgot to turn it on before you went for the vegetables, and put everything together. By the time you've done everything, the recipe will take a lot more than half an hour—at least in the beginning.

I always used to put spaghetti on the table twenty minutes later than I meant to because I didn't allow for the time it took to get the spaghetti pot from the back of the cupboard and bring that huge pot of water to a boil. To partially solve this problem, always turn your oven on to preheat before you do almost anything else. Or put water on to boil. If it boils before you need it, take it off the burner; it will still come to a boil more quickly when you are ready for it.

Next, prepare *all* your ingredients to the cooking stage—dice, blanch, salt, measure, etc.—so that everything is ready to cook, and arranged on little squares of wax paper or in small bowls. Allow plenty of time for browning things. It doesn't matter if browned food cools a little; you can always keep it hot in a 200° F oven on a piece of foil. If you need rice, plan to have it ready a little ahead of time. It will become drier and be much better if it cools off just a little.

A recipe that might be a little tricky or

confusing is best tackled with the phone off the hook.

## USING AN OVEN

If you have an oven with a thermostat that works, you don't have a problem. The following chart will tell you what recipes mean when they say "in a slow oven," etc.:

| | |
|---|---|
| very slow oven | 250-275° F |
| slow oven | 300-325° F |
| moderate oven | 350-375° F |
| hot oven | 400-450° F |
| very hot oven | 475° F and up |

*Check out an oven you are using for the first time.* Buy an inexpensive portable oven thermometer in any hardware store and set it on the middle oven shelf. Then turn your oven on, setting the thermostat to 350° F. When the light goes off, quickly check the reading on the portable thermometer. It should read 350° F. If it does not, make a note of the discrepancy and adjust your oven setting accordingly whenever you cook in it. Many perfectly good ovens are about 50° F off their thermostat settings. If your oven is temperamental, use a portable thermometer regularly instead of relying on the thermostat.

*Always use a meat thermometer for roasts*, except poultry. Regardless of whether your oven works or not, insert a meat thermometer into the center of the raw roast; be careful not to touch bone or get the point into a fatty part. The thermometer has a gauge which tells you when the meat is done. Since roasts vary in cooking time due to size, shape, how cold they are to start with, etc., this is your only reliable guide. It will get your meat just as rare or as well-done as you like it every time.

## USING CERTAIN FOODS

### Cheese

There are thousands of cheeses but they group into three basic categories: soft, semihard, and hard. Cream and cottage cheese are soft; munster is semihard; cheddar, Swiss, and all grating cheeses are hard.

Soft cheese spoils quickly but hard cheese will keep for ages if tightly wrapped and put in the refrigerator. If hard cheese gets moldy, it doesn't spoil it. Just cut off the actual mold and eat the rest. If it's gotten dried out, just grate it and sprinkle it over something.

Cheeses which depend on molds for their flavor (Roquefort, blue, Stilton) can still get *too* moldy. Examine these cheeses before you buy them; get to know which have reached just the right degree of mold. Compare the ones in back of the case with the ones in front. Since they are among the more expensive cheeses, they may sit on the store shelf longer than they should. A good dairy department manager in a supermarket automatically puts the older cheeses in front; sometimes a comparison of the front and back of the case of cheese packages is very educational. Overmoldy cheeses won't hurt you, but they won't taste very good either.

Cheeses are a very valuable food; they contain all the nutrients of milk (except that cream cheese is lower in protein) and are a comparatively inexpensive source of good quality protein. For this reason you should add cheese to your vegetable dishes often, especially if you are a vegetarian. A broiled tomato with a sprinkling of grated cheese or a thin slice of mozzarella is immensely better nutritionally than just plain tomato. Cheese doesn't take kindly to very high temperatures. It will melt better if you don't let it get *too* hot.

## Heavy Cream

Heavy cream will whip better if it is still sweet but not too fresh. A little salt or sugar will help it hold its shape.

## Chocolate

Not all chocolate is sweet. If it is called "cooking chocolate," it is unsweetened or "bitter" chocolate. Make sure you buy the type the recipe calls for. Melt milk chocolate in coffee instead of in water and you will have mocha.

*To grate chocolate.* Chill thoroughly first.

*To melt "cooking chocolate."* Put in the top of a double boiler and melt over hot but *not boiling* water. If the water is boiling, the steam may condense on the cover and drip back into the pan of chocolate. Even a little water will spoil cooking chocolate.

## Eggs

Eggs are comparatively delicate and should not be cooked with high heat unless you want to make them tough. Never salt scrambled eggs or fried eggs until you are serving them. Salting them during cooking will toughen them. Cold eggs separate most easily. Eggs at room temperature whip best.

Dishes, pans, forks, etc., which you have used for mixing, cooking, or eating eggs should be soaked in *cold* water before washing. Hot water will "set" the egg and make it much more difficult to clean off.

Store eggs in the refrigerator large end up. Ideally, they should be covered. The box they come in from the store is a good way to keep them in the refrigerator. If you make a recipe that uses only egg whites, put the yolks, covered with cold water, in a tightly covered jar and store in the refrigerator.

## Baked Ham

Comes two ways: cooked and uncooked. Always ask the butcher which you are buying, unless cooking directions are on the package.

Put the ham on your rack fat side up and it will baste itself. Put 1″ of water in bottom of pan so fat will not get smoking hot or spatter.

## Lettuce and Other Salad Greens

Tear instead of cut for a tossed salad. Salad greens should always be quite dry or the oil will not cling to them properly. In adding oil and vinegar to a tossed salad, always add the oil first. Toss to coat all the ingredients; then add vinegar and toss again.

## Meat

*To store.* Raw meat should be refrigerated loosely wrapped. Always remove meat from the store's wrapping, put on a dish, and lightly cover with wax paper.

Cooked meat should be cooled, then tightly covered and refrigerated as soon as possible after cooking.

*To broil.* Pork chops, etc. won't curl up when broiling if you slash the fat all around the edge at 1″ intervals. This works with bacon, too, but I don't think it's worth the trouble.

Before putting any food in the broiler, turn on the dial setting to "broil" and preheat for 10 minutes. It's a good idea to heat your broiling pan at the same time. Put a piece of foil in the pan under the rack to catch the fat. To test for doneness, make a tiny slit in the meat near the bone and look at it. Broiling time varies with the thickness of the cut, the size of the fish or chicken, etc.

*Never salt meat before broiling.* The salt draws out the juices and makes it dry and tasteless. Turn broiling meat with tongs, not with a fork. A fork will make holes in the seared surface and the juices will run out. Pan broiling works with slices of meat less than 1″ thick. Ideally you should use a skillet you can preheat. After turning, lower the temperature slightly.

Use thick pork chops for baking, thin ones for pan-frying.

## OILS FOR COOKING

Butter adds a nice flavor but burns at a comparatively low temperature. However, clarified butter (see cooking terms) will get much hotter before burning. If a recipe calls for melted butter or shortening, always measure *before* melting.

Peanut, corn, and sesame seed oils will not burn until they reach a comparatively high temperature.

Safflower oil gets rancid fairly quickly so try to buy it in small quantities.

Olive oil adds the most flavor of the vegetable oils because it is the least refined. Virgin oil is the most flavorful of olive oils because it is not refined at all. The flavor varies depending on whether it is French, Italian, or Spanish, but most of the olive oil you use is Italian; the French is very expensive. The flavor enhances a dish, but there are times when you don't want an olive-oil flavor—in frying eggs for breakfast, for instance—so don't use it indiscriminately. Olive oil will solidify if stored in the refrigerator.

# A TABLE OF SUBSTITUTIONS

This is a table that will help you in substituting one ingredient for another in a recipe. You will find it handy when you are missing an ingredient called for but think maybe you have something that will do just as well (e.g. dry herbs for fresh herbs); or you may prefer one ingredient to another (rye flour to white flour, for instance). Substitutions are not foolproof, however. Generally speaking, honey can be substituted for sugar if you adjust the liquid in the recipe, but there are many different kinds of honey and you may want to use more or less depending on the type. In addition, you have to take into account differences in color, texture, and flavor that will occur as you change ingredients. Although it is possible to use cornmeal and white flour interchangeably in some recipes, the resulting finished products will be very different. It's also fun to experiment and discover your own variations; in any case, think of this table as a beginning, not as an infallible guide.

| | |
|---|---|
| 1 FRESH GARLIC CLOVE | ½ teaspoon garlic powder |
| 1 TEASPOON FRESH GINGER | ½ teaspoon ground ginger |
| 1 TABLESPOON FRESH HERBS | ½ to 1 ½ teaspoons dried herbs |
| 1 OUNCE COOKING CHOCOLATE | 3 tablespoons cocoa plus 1 tablespoon oil |
| 1 CUP WHITE SUGAR | 1 cup well-packed brown sugar<br>2 cups corn syrup and reduce liquid in recipe<br>¾ cup honey and reduce liquid in recipe<br>1 ½ cups maple syrup and reduce liquid in recipe<br>1 ½ cups molasses and reduce liquid in recipe |
| 1 CUP WHITE RICE | 1 cup brown rice and allow more liquid and longer cooking time |
| 1 CUP ALL-PURPOSE WHITE FLOUR | 1 cup unbleached white flour<br>1 cup rye flour<br>1 cup wholewheat flour<br>⅓ cup soybean flour plus ⅔ cup all-purpose flour<br>1 cup and 2 tablespoons cake flour<br>⅞ cup rice flour<br>1 cup cornmeal |

| | |
|---|---|
| 1 CUP FRESH MILK | ½ cup evaporated milk plus ½ cup water |
| | ¼ cup dry milk solids plus ¾ cup water |
| | ½ cup condensed milk plus ½ cup water and less sugar than the recipe calls for. To make 1 cup sour milk: add 1 tablespoon vinegar or lemon juice to enough milk so that together they make 1 cup of liquid. Allow to stand 5 minutes. |
| 1 CUP BUTTER | ⅞ cup corn or peanut oil |
| | 1 cup margarine |
| 1 CUP YOGURT | 1 cup buttermilk |
| 1 TEASPOON BAKING POWDER (TARTRATE OR PHOSPHATE) | ⅔ teaspoon double action baking powder |
| | ¼ teaspoon baking soda plus ½ teaspoon cream of tartar |
| | ¼ teaspoon baking soda plus ⅓ cup molasses |
| | *Note*: When the recipe calls for baking powder, use exactly the one specified. There are three kinds and they act differently. If you use the wrong kind, your recipe may not work. |
| 1 TABLESPOON FLOUR (as a thickener) | ½ tablespoon cornstarch |
| | 2 teaspoons quick cooking tapioca |
| | ½ tablespoon arrowroot |
| | *Note*: All of the above ingredients, if used correctly, will satisfactorily thicken the liquid to which they are added; but they produce different results. For instance, flour makes an opaque liquid (like a standard brown gravy); cornstarch makes a translucent sauce (like Chinese gravies); minute tapioca can always be detected by its tiny clear globules. The only way to become familiar with these different results is to try the thickeners; then you will know the one best suited to the results you want to achieve with any given recipe. |

# HERBS, SEEDS, AND SPICES

When I asked students in colleges throughout the country what spices they used in their cooking, I ended up with a list of forty-two different ones. Many answers weren't counted because they said simply "all of them." "We firmly believe," one wrote, expressing the opinion of many, "that using wines and spices in cooking can make the most inexpensive meats much, much better tasting." Vegetarians, too, used wines and spices generously. Even one of the few students who does not use spices said he used "honey and sea salt only," which somehow seems to open up many flavorsome possibilities. However, you indicated you wanted to know even more about herbs and spices than you already do. You asked, in particular, for information as to what to use with what foods. So I have divided this chapter into two parts:

1. A listing of herbs, spices, and seeds most commonly used with some general information about them.
2. A short list of some vegetables and meats and what spices, herbs, and seeds go with them. This is not meant to be used as an inflexible rule, merely as a guide until you can invent your own combinations.

## General Hints

No recipe can really tell you *exactly* how much seasoning to use. Individual tastes vary too much. Even simple seasonings like salt and pepper cannot be pinned down. That is why so many recipes say "salt and pepper to taste." No matter how famous its chef, no restaurant would dare omit the salt and pepper shakers from its tables.

It is always safer to use too little seasoning than too much. When increasing the amount of seasoning in a recipe, increase a very, very little at a time.

Some herbs and spices are delicate and lose flavor with prolonged cooking. If the recipe says to add something toward the end of the cooking period, take this seriously. Otherwise you may cook out all the flavor you think you are adding. Once in a while, but very rarely, a spice gets stronger the more you cook it.

Always taste a dish just before it is done. You can usually correct the seasoning at that point, especially if it is too bland. If you have oversalted, you are in trouble. Try adding two or three potatoes, quartered, and cooking for about 10 or 15 more minutes. Then remove the potatoes. If you are lucky, the salt will come out, too.

Buy good quality herbs and in small amounts. Keep them out of the sun and away from the heat of the stove in airtight containers. Don't pay for fancy packaging each time. Invest in good containers and keep refilling them.

Salts (celery, garlic, etc.) are dried, powdered

herbs and spices mixed with common table salt. Powders (garlic powder, etc.) are not mixed with salt and are, therefore, much more concentrated. I find it easier to use salts because I usually use it without measuring, like sprinkling on hamburgers, and I don't have to be as careful about how much I use. If you use garlic salt when the recipe calls for fresh garlic, cut down on the amount of salt indicated. Taste to tell how much.

*Bouquet garni* and *fines herbes* are two different combinations of herbs. *Bouquet garni* is generally a bay leaf, some parsley, and thyme. *Fines herbes* are frequently parsley, chives, chervil, and a little tarragon. The combination should be wrapped in a piece of cheesecloth, tied securely with a string, and lowered into the liquid of whatever you are cooking. When the dish is done, remove the bag of seasonings. I prefer to have the bits of herbs floating around, but if you want a perfectly clear consommé, for instance, that would not do.

**ALLSPICE.** Derives its name from the fact that its pungent smell and taste are like nutmeg, cinnamon, and cloves all mixed together. If you like it, use it with almost everything from stew to dessert. It is also good with vegetables such as carrots, squash, turnips and with cooked fruit and puddings. Goes with tomato juice, tomato dishes, all meats, poultry (and soups made with them). Use about ¼ teaspoon to 2 quarts of liquid or to an average casserole.

**ANISE.** If you think of this as licorice, you won't go far wrong since it is used to give a licorice flavor to cookies and cakes. You can use ¼-½ teaspoon in the average recipe (to one cup of liquid or to sprinkle over a salad, for instance). It is interesting mixed with stewed fruit, added to fruit juices, and adds a pleasant flavor to chicken or rice—cottage cheese and yogurt, too. Don't use it combined with other spices unless you are very sure it will blend with them.

**BASIL.** This happens to be one of my favorites and I almost never use tomatoes in an Italian recipe without it. To see what a perfect combination that is, try broiled tomatoes (tomatoes cut in half and stuck under a broiler for 10 minutes) both with and without a sprinkling of basil. (I also add a little garlic salt and grated cheese.) Broiled tomatoes with basil is the simple sort of dish that will give you a reputation as a good cook without any work on your part. Another simple, reputation-making dish is tomatoes sliced thick and arranged on a plate with alternate slices of very thin mozzarella. Drizzle olive oil and vinegar over it, sprinkle with basil and salt, and serve as if you were handing around rubies and pearls. Basil is also good with zucchini, peas, eggplant, and stews. It has a delicate flavor and can be used a little more freely than some herbs.

**BAY LEAF.** This is the old-fashioned herb which is especially traditional for stews. You usually take the large flat leaf out just before serving the cooked dish. One leaf is usually enough. It is good, also, with many sauces and with vegetable soup. It isn't used much, however, with boiled vegetables.

**CARAWAY.** These are the seeds you find in rye bread. They are great with boiled cabbage or hot sauerkraut, and, if added to the water in which you are boiling shrimp, will cut down on the shrimp smell. Use them fairly freely in cheese dishes, salads, white sauces, and soups; sprinkle over boiled carrots, onions, and turnips. Mixed with softened butter, they make a nice spread for wheat crackers or whole wheat bread topped with cucumbers and sour cream.

**CARDAMOM.** Unless you have a very complete spice shelf, you probably won't have this. Cinnamon will take its place most of the time or you can use cardamom wherever you would cinnamon. If you want to know exactly what the difference is, mix a little of each with a little sugar and sprinkle on a corner of buttered toast to taste.

**CAYENNE.** This is colorful and *hot*. It is made from dried, ground chili peppers. Use it whenever you want a bit of excitement in deviled eggs, guacamole, cheese dishes, broiled chicken, or shrimp. But use it *very* sparingly, especially if you have guests.

**CELERY SALT.** See "Celery Seed." This is just ground celery seed mixed with table salt.

**CELERY SEED.** A very useful seed when you don't have fresh celery handy. It isn't celery at all but it tastes as if it were and is great in soups, juices, omelets, stews, and with chicken dishes. Use any place you'd like a touch of celery flavoring and use fairly freely.

**CHILI POWDER.** A mixture of spices which varies according to the manufacturer. It comes "hot" and "mild," so buy according to your preference. Chili powder gives the characteristic taste to the mixture of kidney beans and ground beef which we call "chili." You can also use it for dips and to sprinkle over broiled meats, add to a marinade, or put in a casserole. Some people like it with tomato and eggplant dishes. You either like it or you don't, so go easy if you aren't familiar with the flavor. To make a mild chili hotter, add a little cayenne.

**CHIVES.** They are a very mild form of onion that can be easily grown in your kitchen window, handy for chopping up in scrambled eggs, sauces, soups, salads, and to mix with cottage cheese. The green color adds eye appeal and the onion taste is subtle and agreeable.

**CINNAMON.** Almost everyone knows what cinnamon tastes like. It can be used wherever you like it. Use in apple pie, (except *green* apple pie), stewed fruit and, in stick form, for stirring hot cider—also with carrots, sweet potatoes, winter squash, and in all chocolate dishes. It is interesting in cranberry juice and, mixed with sugar, *essential* for cinnamon toast. You can get tired of it, though, so use judgment.

**CLOVES.** Most people have eaten baked ham studded with cloves and know its delightful fragrance. If you add four whole cloves to two quarts of chicken broth, you will have a delicious soup. An onion studded with cloves is an easy way to flavor stew. It's good with all ham and pork dishes, with carrots, yams, squash, onions, and many desserts and cooked fruits. Try it in tea.

**CURRY POWDER.** Some people make their own, but most prefer to buy this mixture of spices ready-made. Like chili, curry powders vary considerably from mild to hot and can be very, very hot indeed. What makes it hot is good old cayenne pepper, so add a little if your curry is too mild. If you like curry, add it to a white sauce and pour over any combination of cooked meat, fish, or leftover vegetables to serve on hot rice. Don't use more than ½ to 1 teaspoon for a 6-serving recipe until you find out how much you like. It is good in pea soup and is the primary seasoning in mulligatawny soup. A good cheap meal is hot hard-cooked eggs sliced over hot rice with a curried sauce poured over the whole thing.

**DILL.** This is an herb appreciated more in Scandinavia than here, which is too bad. Fresh dill, minced and sprinkled over boiled potatoes (the way you do parsley) adds a Scandinavian flavor and turns an ordinary dish into something special. Dill is good with anything you cook or serve with sour cream (except sweet things or fruit), potato salad, seafood, creamed foods, and, of course, for pickling.

**GARLIC.** This is my favorite of all herbs, and sooner or later I use it in almost everything except desserts—in soups, stews, casseroles, sauces, salads, and garlic bread. Not everyone shares my enthusiasm, however, so go easy. Garlic salt in salad won't leave an odor on the breath the way fresh garlic will. Sometimes that is a consideration. A fresh garlic clove is much better than garlic salt if you have the time to work with it. For just a hint of flavor in a tossed salad, rub it on bread cubes and toss the cubes in the salad with your dressing. Remove cubes before serving salad. Garlic salt is good sprinkled (sparingly) on hamburgers or broiled chicken.

**GINGER.** A spice that's fun to use unexpectedly because it's almost always pleasant and hard to figure out. Try it in a simple, basic macaroni and cheese recipe or with hot, buttered carrots or yams. Add it to apple dishes and juices; mix with cream cheese for a spread. If you make a cup of chicken broth, stir in a little ginger. Try it with plain yogurt. This is one spice you can improvise with.

**MARJORAM.** This is a gentle relative of oregano. Because it is one of the more aromatic herbs, don't use more than ½ teaspoon to 6 servings. It is very versatile and can be used in just about everything from spreads to stews. Try it where you feel the need for a new taste. Chances are you won't actively dislike it no matter what you cook it with—even scrambled eggs.

**MINT.** Of course you know what mint tastes like. But you might not think to sprinkle it on green peas, carrots or soups made from these vegetables. Add it to juices and cooked fruit; sprinkle in salads.

**NUTMEG.** It is sweet and fragrant sprinkled over rice pudding—tasty with onions, tomatoes, or green beans. Try it in something unexpected. Just taste a little on the tip of your finger to see what you're dealing with.

**OREGANO.** The spice that makes pizzas what they are. It's strong and should be used sparingly. All tomato and most meat dishes like it—so do broccoli, eggplant, dried bean casseroles, and eggs. Try ¼ teaspoon to 6 servings. Add to broths for drinking or cooking.

**PAPRIKA.** So colorful that many dishes call for it just for its decorative quality. It makes broiled chicken look elegant and, of course, is traditionally added in great quantities to Hungarian dishes. If you want to make it hot, add cayenne. A little sprinkled on broiled fish gives it a company look. It is good with cauliflower. If you use just a little, the flavor will not be too obtrusive; if you want to use a lot, and are sure you like the flavor, use it freely.

**PARSLEY.** An herb which adds vitamins, minerals, color, and an invariably pleasing flavor. Add it just before serving, when possible, to get the most nutrients out of it. It can be served whole with just the stem removed or minced. Mix it with salads, cottage cheese, all soups, and any sauce—an easy way to make scrambled eggs look like company fare. Toss with hot, boiled noodles and cottage cheese for a quick, inexpensive, and healthful supper or stir into sour cream or yogurt with a little lemon juice and you have a good salad dressing. You simply can't go wrong with parsley no matter how much or how little you use.

**POPPY SEEDS.** An interesting way to add a nutlike flavor to hot, buttered noodles or rice. It is good, too, with carrots, summer squash, cabbage, green beans. Mix with cottage cheese or cream cheese. Also used for baking, of course.

**ROSEMARY.** It smells so good that it was once used (like pine needles) to stuff pillows and scent soap. Don't use too much of it, though. It is good with seafood and baked chicken. I like it in tomato dishes and stews, also. Just use ½ teaspoon for the average recipe for 6.

**SAFFRON.** This has the dubious honor of being the most expensive of all spices. So naturally, there are imitations to beware of. If you buy a thimbleful (the way it is often sold), be sure it is the real thing. Use very sparingly—a little goes a long way. It turns rice a lovely yellow color (for paella, etc.) and adds a pleasant, offbeat flavor to chicken and egg dishes. If all you want is the color, use turmeric instead; it's lots cheaper and has an interesting taste.

**SAGE.** This is the very strong and pungent odor that used to come from your grandmother's roasting turkey. No self-respecting Colonial stuffing would have been made without it. Use very little but you can try it with anything from pork to cheese dishes—even stuffed cabbage.

**SESAME.** I think you probably use more sesame seeds than any generation of cooks for centuries. They are best toasted (which gives them a nuttier flavor), and can be added wherever you would use nuts. Sprinkle them on vegetables, mix them with butter or cream cheese, add them to salads, chicken, and noodles. To toast, put them in a 350° F oven for 25 minutes or until they have turned a pale brown color. Be sure they are spread over the pan so that they do not lie one over the other.

**TARRAGON.** If I had to say what this tastes like, I would say licorice, but there is a subtle difference that makes it good for flavoring vinegar, baked chicken, and sauces. Don't use too much of it, but try it with carrots, onions, and tomatoes. Capers are traditionally bottled in tarragon vinegar, so when you add them to salads, use the liquid, too.

THYME. Start with ¼ teaspoon to a recipe for 6 as this is fairly strong in flavor. It is essential in fish stews; try it also with meat stew, carrots, squash, onions, tomato juice, or mix with cottage or cream cheese to scramble with eggs.

TURMERIC. It is basically mustardy in taste. Adds a lovely golden orange color to sauces or rice. Start with ¼ teaspoon for 6 servings and increase to taste and color desired. Turmeric is good with chicken dishes and creamed recipes.

## SEASONING SUGGESTIONS

This list is meant only to suggest possibilities, not to exhaust them. Do not lose sight of the fact that food tastes good in itself. Too many spices spoil rather than enhance a dish. But the right spice in the right dish is a lovely thing.

(one at a time unless you are *sure*)

**Avocado:** cayenne, garlic, chili powder
**Beans, dried:** oregano, parsley
**Beans, green:** nutmeg, parsley, poppy seeds, sesame seeds
**Broccoli:** oregano
**Cabbage:** caraway seeds, poppy seeds, sesame seeds
**Carrots:** allspice, caraway seeds, cinnamon, cloves, dill, ginger, mint, parsley, poppy seeds, tarragon, thyme
**Cauliflower:** paprika, parsley, sesame seeds
**Cheese:** caraway, cayenne, parsley, poppy seeds, sesame seeds, thyme, nutmeg
**Cottage cheese:** anise, chives, parsley, sesame seeds
**Eggplant:** basil, chili, garlic, oregano
**Eggs:** cayenne, celery seed, chives, curry, dill, oregano, parsley, thyme, turmeric
**Fish:** curry, dill, paprika, parsley, rosemary, thyme, garlic
**Ham:** cloves

**Lamb:** curry, garlic, mint, parsley, rosemary
**Meats:** allspice, chili, curry, garlic
**Onions:** caraway, cloves, curry, nutmeg, tarragon, thyme
**Peas:** basil, cloves, mint, parsley
**Potatoes:** dill, parsley
**Poultry:** allspice, curry, garlic, ginger, parsley, sesame seeds, anise, cayenne, celery seed, rosemary
**Rice:** turmeric, saffron, curry, anise, garlic, parsley, poppy seeds, sesame seeds
**Squash, winter:** allspice, cinnamon, cloves, ginger, thyme
**Stews:** allspice, basil, bay leaf, cloves, garlic, parsley, oregano, thyme
**Tomatoes:** allspice, basil, chili, dill, garlic, nutmeg, oregano, parsley, tarragon, thyme
**Turnips:** allspice, caraway seeds
**Yams or sweet potatoes:** cinnamon, cloves, ginger
**Yogurt:** anise, ginger, mint
**Zucchini:** basil, garlic

# SOUP

**Recipes included and the chief ingredients needed.**

ALICE'S STOCKPOT
Leftovers, scraps, etc.

PETER'S CABBAGE SOUP
Cabbage, potatoes, carrots, onions, turnip, olive oil, tomato paste

SIMPLE VEGETABLE SOUP
Carrots, zucchini (or cabbage), canned tomatoes, turnips, celery, onions, potatoes, kidney beans, pasta

NANNY'S CHICKEN SOUP
Chicken, carrots, onions, celery, parsnips, potatoes

NEW ENGLAND COD CHOWDER
Chowder cod, potatoes, onion, milk

CREAM OF ONION SOUP
Onions, carrot, heavy cream, milk

GAZPACHO
Cucumbers, onion, carrots, radishes, pimientos, green chili salsa, dill, lemons, tomatoes, and tomato juice

HOT FRUIT SOUP
Apples, peaches, cherries, plums, sour cream

LYNN'S VEGETABLE-BEEF SOUP
Soup bone, beef, potatoes, onions, carrots

SPLIT PEA SOUP
Dried split peas, bacon, onions, celery

WENDY'S LENTIL SOUP
Lentils, onion, carrots, celery, tomato paste, parsley

REAL FRENCH ONION SOUP
Olive oil, onion, flour, beef stock, oregano, white wine

FRESH TOMATO SOUP
Tomatoes, cloves, onion, flour

SPINACH EGG DROP SOUP
Onion, celery, spinach, bouillon cubes, egg, Parmesan cheese

SUPER BROCCOLI SOUP
Onion, celery, potatoes, chicken broth, broccoli, herbs

POTATO ANYTHING SOUP
Onion, celery, potatoes, carrots

COLD CUCUMBER SOUP
Cucumber, garlic, dill, mint, yogurt

# SOUP

If you're not already a soup buff, you're missing out on a good thing. Soup is cheap, filling, nutritious, delicious, and very, very easy to make. It's also good for feeding large groups of people with no fuss (and only one pot to clean). Several students on the West Coast wrote me that they use a Japanese instant soup and like it very much. If you can find miso soup, it has interesting ingredients and is a change from bouillon cubes. Anyone who can simmer water can make homemade soup. Just take a mixture of vegetables, cut them up fairly small, simmer for 20 minutes, add salt and pepper, a pat of butter, a bouillon cube and presto—soup!

Traditionally, making soup began with a stockpot. This was a big pot that stood on the back of the coal stove and simmered away constantly. Whatever was available—cooking water from vegetables, peelings, scraps, bones, etc. was dumped into it each day. Nothing was ever wasted, including vitamins and minerals which today we often toss into the garbage. Obviously, the flavor was never the same twice, and it wasn't meant to be eaten just as it was; but it formed a nutritious, tasty stock or base for an endless variety of fine soups. It was almost as handy as opening a can.

UNIVERSITY OF COLORADO
# Alice's Stockpot

Keep large jar in refrigerator for leftovers, drained juices, cooked vegetables, etc.—the nutritious part we usually throw away. When full, heat and serve as it is or use as a base for soup or stew. If you don't use it all, dump it in a pan and simmer for 10 minutes once a week or it will go sour.

UNIVERSITY OF MICHIGAN
# Peter's Cabbage Soup

1 pound potatoes, sliced
2 quarts water
1 cabbage, shredded
4 carrots, sliced
3 onions, chopped
1 turnip, diced
¼ cup olive oil
½ small can tomato paste
salt to taste

Boil potatoes in water. When tender, mash in the cooking water. Add all other ingredients. Simmer, covered, for 1-1½ hours. You may need to add more water to keep this soup from getting too thick, but it should be substantial and hearty.
Serves: 4

COLUMBIA UNIVERSITY
# Simple Vegetable Soup

*A good soup to study by. Fixing the vegetables is sort of restful; it smells good cooking, and it is a meal in itself without being heavy. It's cheap, too.*

½ cup each, diced: carrots, turnips, zucchini (optional), canned tomatoes, celery, onions, potatoes
1 cup kidney beans, canned or cooked
1 cup elbow macaroni (or any other pasta), cooked or raw
2 quarts boiling water
½ teaspoon basil
1 tablespoon butter
salt and pepper to taste

Heat butter in frying pan and toss diced vegetables in it. Cook quickly, stirring constantly, for 5 minutes. Add to boiling water, along with beans, pasta, and basil. Bring to boil and simmer 20 minutes. Add salt and pepper. For a richer soup, use less water or add more of everything. If you don't have zucchini, use shredded cabbage.
Serves: 6-8

BOSTON UNIVERSITY

# Nanny's Chicken Soup

*You've heard of "have a little chicken soup." This is the soup. Easy and tasty, and you can improvise.*

**1 chicken, cut in parts**
**½ cup carrots, diced**
**½ cup onions, diced**
**½ cup celery, chopped**
**½ cup parsnips, diced**
**½ cup potatoes, diced**

Put chicken and first three vegetables in cold water to cover and bring to boil. Cook 30 minutes on low heat. Add salt to taste. Add last two vegetables and cook 30 minutes more. Add more salt, if necessary (this soup needs a good amount), and serve. **Serves: 6**

UNIVERSITY OF VERMONT

# New England Cod Chowder

*This is traditional and I try to make it often because it is cheap and filling.*

**2 pounds chowder cod (very, very cheap)**
**5 potatoes**
**2 cups boiling water**
**1 onion, sliced**
**2 cups milk**
**¼ pound butter**
**salt and pepper to taste**

Put cod in a bowl of cold, salted water. It sometimes has tiny worms in it and this will make them float to the top where you can pour them off. (If the thought bothers you, forget the cod and use clams instead.) Peel and dice potatoes. Boil 5 minutes in 2 cups of boiling water in a large pot. Put fish in 1 cup cold water, bring to boil, and simmer 10 minutes. Strain broth. Bone cod. Add cod and broth to potatoes and potato water, with the onion. Simmer 20 minutes. Add milk, season with salt and pepper, and heat until it starts to form little bubbles (*very* soon). Serve with a pat of butter in each soup dish. **Serves: 3-4**

UNIVERSITY OF NEW HAMPSHIRE

# Cream of Onion Soup

*Most any vegetable can be turned into a cream soup. We like this one, but you can substitute asparagus, carrots, or any other vegetable that you want.*

2 large onions
1 tablespoon carrot, grated
3 tablespoons butter
3 tablespoons flour
2 quarts boiling water
1 bouillon cube
2 cups hot milk
½ cup heavy cream
1 teaspoon Worcestershire sauce
salt and pepper to taste

Boil onions 5 minutes, drain and finely chop. Melt butter, blend in flour, and cook for 1 minute, stirring constantly. Add boiling water, bouillon cube, grated carrot, and simmer for 5 minutes. Add hot milk and cream, Worcestershire sauce, salt and pepper to taste, and heat just to boiling point. If you want it perfectly smooth, put in blender just before adding milk and cream. **Serves: 6**

VASSAR COLLEGE

# Gazpacho

*You need a blender for this one, and you don't cook it.*

2 cucumbers
1 large can tomato juice
2 carrots
5 radishes
1 Spanish onion
2 lemons
1 jar of pimientos
1 can green chili salsa (optional—makes it hot)
2 tablespoons fresh dill weed
herbs you like—sweet basil, oregano, coriander, thyme
3 teaspoons black pepper
1 ½ teaspoons garlic powder
1 ripe tomato

Peel the cucumbers, but not completely. Cut them in small pieces. Add one cucumber at a time (blenders don't like large amounts). Add some tomato juice (makes the blender work more easily) and blend until pulp. Pour into large container. Don't use metal! Repeat with carrots, radishes, and any other vegetable you like. Do the same with ½ the onion. The rest you dice and just put in at the end. Add the juice of 2 lemons and the rest of the tomato juice. Add pimientos and salsa. Mix. Add spices. Slice the tomato and add. Refrigerate. It's best after a couple of hours when things get together, and better as days go by. It's refreshing, and filling. **Serves: 6-8**

Barnard College
# Hot Fruit Soup

*Buy leftover fruit, not perfect, late Saturday afternoon. This is the fruit I used last time, but I buy what the market has, so it's not always the same.*

1½ quarts cold water
1 cup apples, unpeeled, cored, and quartered
1 cup peaches, unpeeled, halved
1 cup cherries
1 cup plums, unpeeled, halved
1 stick cinnamon
1 clove
1 cup sour cream
2 tablespoons flour
2 tablespoons sugar

Put fruit, cinnamon, and clove in pan with 1½ quarts of cold water. Bring to boil and simmer 25 minutes. Strain the fruit from the soup and remove pits. Mash fruit or puree in blender. Add enough water to make 1½ quarts of soup. Add fruit pulp. Bring to boil. Mix flour with sour cream and stir into boiling soup. Add sugar. Bring to a boil again and serve. Good poured over hot, freshly cooked boiled potatoes in a big soup bowl. **Serves: 4**

University of Colorado
# Lynn's Vegetable-Beef Soup

*This recipe doesn't give amounts of everything because it isn't critical. Figure on 4-5 cups of vegetables altogether in any combination depending on what you have. Basically, as long as you have meat, potatoes, and vegetables, you are all right.*

2 quarts cold water
1 soup bone
1 pound beef cut in medium-sized chunks (or a very meaty soup bone)
potatoes, peeled and cut into chunks
onions, cut up, or small ones whole
carrots, sliced
leftover vegetables or meat
½ teaspoon sage
½ teaspoon rosemary
1 bay leaf (remove before serving)

Put all ingredients in water and bring to boil. Turn down and let simmer. Make it in the morning and simmer it all day—at least for 5 hours. Serve with homemade bread. **Serves: Depends on quantity**

SCHOOL OF THE MUSEUM OF FINE ARTS

# Split Pea Soup

*A jar of this in the refrigerator beats coffee as a pick-me-up at 4:00 A.M. before the big exam. It won't let you down right in the middle either.*

1 pound dried split peas
1 pound bacon, uncooked
4 onions, diced
2 stalks celery, diced
2½ quarts cold water
salt and pepper to taste

Throw all the ingredients in the cold water and simmer until peas disappear or get mushy—usually 3 hours. Add water during cooking if necessary to keep it from getting *too* thick. Remove bacon from pot, dry on paper towels, and fry until crisp. Crumble into soup and serve whenever you like. **Serves: 4-6**

MIDDLEBURY COLLEGE

# Wendy's Lentil Soup

*Very high in protein and very inexpensive.*

1 cup dried lentils
6 cups water
1 onion, chopped
4 carrots, chopped
2 stalks celery, chopped
½ can tomato paste
chopped parsley
minced garlic
chopped dill
chopped thyme
chopped tarragon
salt and pepper to taste
dry white wine (optional)

Rinse lentils in cold water. Pick over, taking out anything that isn't a lentil. Put first 5 ingredients in a pot and simmer gently for 1-1½ hours, until lentils are tender. If you need to add more water, do so. Add herbs in whatever quantity you like, a little at a time. Add salt and pepper to taste. Stir in tomato paste and reheat. **Serves: 4-6**

COLUMBIA UNIVERSITY

# Real French Onion Soup

3 tablespoons butter
2 tablespoons olive oil
6 cups onions, thinly sliced
2 tablespoons flour
2 quarts beef stock
1 teaspoon salt
1 teaspoon oregano
½ cup white wine (optional)

Heat 1 tablespoon of butter and the olive oil in a soup kettle. Add onions, salt, and oregano and stir to coat with butter and oil. Sauté onions until golden brown, stirring occasionally. Onions should not be allowed to burn, but the deeper golden they are the more flavor the soup will have. Keep an eye on them; they turn color all of a sudden. Sprinkle flour over onions and stir to blend for about 3 minutes. Add beef stock and reheat. Add wine and simmer for 40 minutes, adding the rest of the butter just before serving.

To serve French style, put a thick slice of French bread, topped with grated Parmesan cheese in each filled soup bowl and put under the broiler until the cheese melts. If you don't have Parmesan cheese, any cheese that will melt will work.
**Serves: 6**

MIDDLEBURY COLLEGE

# Fresh Tomato Soup

Boil 6 or more tomatoes (buy the soft ones from your grocer extra cheap) with 6 cloves and a small onion chopped into enough water to cover. When the tomatoes are soft, remove from soup water and strain. Put tomato base aside and strain soup. Reheat tomato base, adding sugar and salt to taste. While it is heating, mix 1 tablespoon of flour into a paste with a little water (if you don't mix it with the water, it will clump in the soup). Add to the tomato base along with ½ the soup water. Simmer until it starts to thicken, stirring occasionally. Add more water and stir until it reaches the degree of thickness you want. Sprinkle with minced parsley and serve.

UNIVERSITY OF NEW HAMPSHIRE

# Spinach Egg Drop Soup

½ large onion, chopped
1 stalk celery, chopped
1 package fresh spinach, washed and chopped
2 tablespoons butter
3-4 cups water
3-4 bouillon cubes
1 egg
1 tablespoon Parmesan cheese, grated

Sauté onion and celery in butter until onion is lightly browned. Add spinach and toss in butter. Lower heat, cover and cook slowly until spinach softens (it will wilt). Add 3-4 cups of water and bouillon cubes. Bring to a gentle, rolling boil. Beat egg and cheese together. Drop egg mixture from spoon into soup slowly in a steady stream, stirring vigorously to keep water swirling. Remove from heat and serve immediately. **Serves: 2**

UNIVERSITY OF NEW HAMPSHIRE

# Super Broccoli Soup

1 large onion, chopped
3 large stalks celery, chopped
2 tablespoons butter
2 large or 3 small potatoes, diced
1 chicken bouillon cube to each cup of water, plus one
1 large head of broccoli, chopped
½ teaspoon basil
1 tablespoon parsley
salt and pepper to taste

Sauté onion and celery in butter until onion is translucent and celery is soft. Add potatoes, toss to coat with butter. Add enough water to cover the potatoes but measure the amount of water as you add it so you will know how many bouillon cubes to put in. Add the bouillon cubes. Cover and simmer 15 minutes. Add broccoli, herbs, and seasonings. Simmer until broccoli is tender (about 10 minutes). Remove ⅓ of the vegetables with a slotted spoon and put in blender. If blender is glass, be sure to warm it with hot water before adding steaming vegetables, or the glass may break. Puree vegetables in the blender and toss back into soup. If a thicker soup is desired, simmer uncovered until consistency is the way you want it. Be sure to stir often. Serve with hot rolls or pita bread sandwiches. **Serves: 2-3**

WESLEYAN UNIVERSITY
# Potato Anything Soup

*As long as you have potatoes, onions, and dried milk, you can make this soup. The milk protein complements the potato; everything else is variable. Save broccoli stalks, slightly wilted carrots, celery, or any bits or pieces of vegetables for this soup. Here's one version:*

1 medium onion, chopped
3 stalks celery, chopped
2 tablespoons butter
4 medium potatoes, chopped
1-2 carrots, grated
1 bay leaf

Sauté onions and celery in butter for 3 minutes. Add potatoes and carrots and cover with water (2-3 cups). Bring to boil. Add bay leaf and simmer approximately 20 minutes, until potatoes are soft. Put ½-¾ of potatoes through blender or mash against sides of pot.

At this point you can add some, none, or all of the following:

**fresh or frozen peas**
**corn**
**broccoli**
**cauliflower**
**zucchini**
**summer squash**

Add water, if necessary, and cook until vegetables are done (between 5-20 minutes, depending on what you added).

⅓ cup non-instant dried milk (or ½ cup i
½ cup water

Mix ingredients. Stir into soup, adding more water if you like soup thinner. Reheat but do not boil. Spoon into soup bowls and garnish with parsley, green onions, or grated cheese. **Serves: Depends on quantity**

**Variations**: Bell pepper sauteed with onions; tomatoes or tomato paste.

UNIVERSITY OF NEW HAMPSHIRE
# Cold Cucumber Soup

1 cucumber, chopped but not peeled
1 teaspoon salt
1-2 garlic cloves, chopped
2 tablespoons dill
1 tablespoon mint
1-1½ cups plain yogurt

Put all ingredients in blender and blend until the consistency you like (small, crunchy bits of cucumber are tasty). Chill in refrigerator until thickened a little. Serve at once. **Serves: 1**

# EGGS

**Recipes included and the chief ingredients needed.**

SOFT-COOKED EGGS
Eggs

HARD-COOKED EGGS
Eggs

FRIED EGGS
Eggs

POACHED EGGS
Eggs

JAMES OMELET
Eggs, onion, green pepper, tomato, milk

HERBED SCRAMBLED EGGS
Eggs, milk or cream, American cheese, herbs

ONION OMELET
Eggs, onion, sour cream

EGG FOO YONG
Eggs, shrimp or chicken (optional), bean sprouts,
green onions, bamboo shoots, water chestnuts,
green peppers

CHINESE EGGS
Eggs, cooked rice, pork, chicken, or ham

EGG SALAD
Eggs, relish, onion

PATTY'S BREAD AND CHEESE CASSEROLE
Eggs, bread, cheese, onions, green pepper,
tomatoes

EGGPLANT EGGS
Eggs, eggplant, tomatoes

HUNGARIAN PALACSINTA
Eggs, milk, flour, butter

CARROT PUDDING
Eggs, carrots, light cream

EGG AND POTATO CASSEROLE
Eggs, potatoes, onions, American cheese, parsley

EGGS RICHARD
Bread, eggs, Swiss cheese

LESLEY'S CHEESE SOUFFLÉ
Eggs, bread, sharp cheddar cheese

CHEESE AND SHRIMP SOUFFLÉ
Shrimp, cheddar cheese, milk, eggs

THE WHATEVER-YOU-HAVE-IN-THE-FRIDGE
QUICHE
Pie crust, cream or milk, eggs, Swiss cheese,
vegetables

CALIFORNIA OMELET
Eggs, powdered sugar, oranges, orange juice,
Grand Marnier

BAKED EGGS IN CREAM
Eggs, heavy cream, bread crumbs, nutmeg

# EGGS

Eggs are useful, tasty, versatile, and very easy on the budget. They are also one of your best sources of protein. For instance, if you are a vegetarian, it is hard to plan meals that provide sufficient protein—even with generous use of dried beans—but if you add eggs to your vegetable dishes, you have no problem. It is better not to buy or use cracked eggs. Eggs are used in laboratories as culture mediums because they are such a good breeding ground for germs. As long as the shell is whole, the contents are clean, but once the shell is cracked, the egg is no longer safe.

Have eggs at room temperature when you are planning to boil them and they will be less liable to crack as you lower them into the water. If you're not sure whether an egg is fresh, drop it in a glass of water. Fresh eggs sink, old eggs float. If you're not sure whether an egg in the refrigerator is hard-boiled or raw, spin it on the countertop. A raw egg will spin in place; a hard-boiled one will spin unevenly all over the top.

A teaspoon of water added to an omelet egg mix will make the omelet more tender because it retards coagulation of the yolks. Here is how to cook basic egg dishes.

### "BOILED" EGGS

The simplest way to cook an egg is to boil it. But eggs are delicate and should never be really "boiled," so we will call them "cooked" and never let the water get hotter than simmer.

**Soft-Cooked Eggs.** This is the kind of egg you eat with a spoon from an egg cup. All you need is a small pan of boiling water with a pinch of salt in it and your eggs. Take the pan off the burner and *slowly* lower the egg into the water with a metal spoon. Set it gently on the bottom of the pan and add the rest of the eggs one at a time.

Then put the pan back on the burner and cook just under boiling (simmer). Depending on how you like your eggs, cook them as follows:

2½ minutes = soft egg
3 minutes = medium egg
4 minutes = egg with a yolk that is mostly hard but with a slightly runny center

**Hard-Cooked Eggs.** Proceed as for soft-cooked but simmer for 10 minutes.

**To peel hard-cooked eggs easily.** As soon as the egg is cooked, put it in ice cold water for a few minutes. Then change the water and put in fresh cold water. Do not let the eggs warm up in the water. When the egg feels cool if held in the hand, it is ready to peel or to put in the refrigerator. It will peel easily if you break the shell all around the widest part of the egg with a knife or the rim of a cup. The shell will pull apart cleanly in two halves.

But if after doing this you still have trouble peeling the eggs cleanly, your eggs are too fresh. Use eggs at least three days old for hard cooking.

## FRIED EGGS

Heat aluminum skillet (if you are using stainless steel, you cannot heat it empty, so heat it with butter already in it) and then add 1 tablespoon butter—just enough to grease the bottom of the skillet so that eggs won't stick. Tilt the pan to get butter all over the bottom. Break eggs into cup or saucer and slide, one at a time, into the butter when it is hot but not burning. Turn heat down slightly and cook until white is solid and yolks are hot. If you are not sure, touch the top of the yolk lightly with your finger. This is called "sunny side up."

If you prefer, you can use more butter and spoon it over the yolk while the egg is cooking. This will turn the yolk opaque. (You can also cover the pan for a minute to get the same result.) If you want the egg for a fried egg sandwich, turn it over with a spatula and brown the other side, breaking the yolk in the process. Otherwise you will have egg on your chin with your first bite. Salt and pepper to taste *after* the egg is cooked.

## POACHED EGGS

Making a good poached egg always gives me a feeling of accomplishment. Especially if you do it the French way, which is to drop the whole egg (broken out of its shell into a cup) into a small pan of boiling salted water. If the egg is really fresh, the white will wrap itself around the yolk and make a reasonably compact mass. Cook it for 3 minutes in gently boiling water and remove with a slotted spoon. An easier way is to buy an egg poacher (they come for one egg or several). In which case, you break the eggs into the buttered metal cups which sit over boiling water. These cups keep the eggs nicely shaped so that they look handsome on a properly golden brown piece of toast.

Poached eggs are very handy. They can be served in a well on top of corned beef hash or hot cooked spinach, or over a piece of broccoli and ham, etc. They will make a breakfast, lunch, or dinner depending on how substantial the other things you serve are. But the quickest, easiest way to cook eggs is to scramble them.

CURTIS INSTITUTE OF MUSIC
# James Omelet

6 eggs
½ cup onion, chopped
½ cup green pepper, chopped
1 tomato, diced
½ cup milk
¼ teaspoon paprika
1 tablespoon butter
salt and pepper to taste

Beat eggs. Add onions, peppers, and tomato. Pour in milk. Flavor with paprika. Pour into hot, buttered skillet and cook for 10 minutes over medium heat. Put under broiler for 3-5 minutes to brown. Replace on top of stove burner. When solidified, remove from heat. Salt and pepper to taste. **Serves: 2-3**

BARNARD COLLEGE
# Herbed Scrambled Eggs

2 eggs
2 tablespoons milk or cream
½ teaspoon chopped chives, dill, or tarragon
1 tablespoon American cheese
1 tablespoon butter

Beat everything together, except butter, lightly with a fork. Heat frying pan, add butter. When foam of butter starts to subside, pour in egg mixture and cook on lowered medium heat, stirring gently with your fork to "scramble." Eggs are done when they look creamy or just firm. Do not cook them dry. The whole cooking time shouldn't take more than 3-4 minutes. **Serves: 1**

YALE UNIVERSITY

# Onion Omelet

3 eggs
1 tablespoon water
½ onion, thinly sliced
2 tablespoons sour cream
1 tablespoon butter
salt and pepper to taste

Break eggs in bowl and add water. Slice onions and separate into rings. Beat eggs and water lightly. Pour into small, hot, buttered skillet. Lift up edges as eggs cook and tilt pan so uncooked egg runs over the sides onto bottom of pan. When eggs are almost set, lay onion all over the top. Cook for a minute more. Just before taking out of pan, spoon sour cream over ½ of the eggs. Fold over with spatula and slide onto plate. Season. The eggs and onions are hot and the sour cream is cold. Great! **Serves: 1**

UNION COLLEGE, SCHENECTADY, NY

# Egg Foo Yong

*Very filling and good—serve with hot rice.*

6 eggs
½ cup shrimp or chicken (optional)
½ cup bean sprouts
1 cup green onions, thinly sliced
½ cup bamboo shoots, thinly sliced
½ cup water chestnuts, thinly sliced
½ cup green peppers, thinly sliced
1 teaspoon salt or 2 teaspoons soy sauce
2 tablespoons peanut oil
¼ teaspoon pepper

Beat eggs thoroughly and add other ingredients, except oil. Mix well and divide into 4 portions. Drop 1 portion into skillet with hot peanut oil. A small skillet is best, since omelet should be small and thick rather than spread out. Butter is all right if you don't have peanut oil. Brown on both sides, turning with spatula. Cook until firm. Keep cooked ones hot and cook one at a time. **Serves: 4**

Gravy (not necessary but good):
2 teaspoons soy sauce
1 teaspoon sugar
1 teaspoon vinegar
½ cup cold water
1 teaspoon cornstarch

We use cornstarch because it keeps the sauce translucent in real Chinese style but you can use any thickener you like. Put all the ingredients in small saucepan and cook over low heat until thick. Pour over each serving of Egg Foo Yong.

UNION COLLEGE, SCHENECTADY, NY

# Chinese Eggs

1 cup minced pork, chicken, or ham
3 cups cooked rice
1 tablespoon butter
6 eggs
2 tablespoons soy sauce

Heat meat and rice in skillet in butter. Add soy sauce. Add beaten eggs and stir all together. Keep stirring and cook until eggs are done. Serves: 3

CURTIS INSTITUTE OF MUSIC

# Egg Salad

6 eggs
1 tablespoon mayonnaise
¼ teaspoon mustard
½ teaspoon relish
½ teaspoon onion, chopped
salt and pepper to taste

Hard-cook 6 eggs. Separate yolks and white and chop. Mix the yolks with mayonnaise and mustard. Add relish, onions, and chopped egg whites. Use more mayonnaise if necessary to bind. Salt and pepper. **Serves: 3**

**Note**: The eggs can be either hot or cold when you use them.

UNIVERSITY OF CALIFORNIAT AT LOS ANGELES

# Patty's Bread and Cheese Casserole

6 slices bread
2 cups grated cheese (cheddar or whatever you like)
2 onions, thinly sliced
1 green pepper, chopped
3 tomatoes, sliced
salt and pepper to taste
½ cup butter
1¼ cups milk
2 eggs

Preheat oven to 350° F. Use sliced wholewheat or leftover bread of any kind—stale or otherwise. Toast and cut into smaller pieces. Put layer of bread, layer of cheese, layer of vegetables. Salt and pepper. Dot with butter or sprinkle with any salad oil, except olive oil, if you don't have butter. Repeat until everything is used up. Heat milk and beat in eggs. Pour over whole thing. Bake for about 40 minutes or until milk has been absorbed and cheese is melted and bubbly. Very good—very easy. Finely chopped green onions are really good in this. **Serves: 3**

MILLS COLLEGE

# Eggplant Eggs

*A really inexpensive dish that tastes expensive. Filling enough for dinner if you serve two to a person.*

8 slices eggplant, about ½″ thick (use small
    eggplant)
3 tablespoons butter
3 tomatoes, thickly sliced (use leftover ends
    and very small slices in salad)
8 eggs
½ cup bread crumbs
salt and pepper to taste

Bread eggplant and sauté in butter until brown. Set aside but keep hot. Grill tomato slices under broiler for 2 minutes on each side, but be sure they do not get soft. If no broiler, dip in bread crumbs and fry quickly in butter for 1 minute on each side. Keep hot. Fry eggs, keeping each one separate from the others. Cover each eggplant slice with a tomato slice (use slices big enough to cover the eggplant) and top with fried egg. Season. This takes only one pan and very little time.
**Serves: 4**

UNIVERSITY OF CONNECTICUT

# Hungarian Palacsinta

*These are what some people call crêpes.*

3 eggs
2 cups milk
1½ cups flour
1 tablespoon confectioner's sugar
½ teaspoon salt
1 tablespoon melted butter
6 teaspoons melted butter

Beat eggs until frothy. Add sugar, 1 tablespoon melted butter, salt, milk, and flour, beating in as you add. Batter must be about the consistency of melted ice cream. Brush pan thickly with melted butter for each "crêpe." When butter is hot, spoon in 2-3 tablespoons of batter and quickly rotate pan so that the batter spreads evenly and thinly over the bottom. A 6″-8″ pan is best. Brown quickly, then turn to brown other side. Stack cooked "crêpes" in a flat dish with waxed paper in between. They can be made in advance and stored in the refrigerator until needed.

To use, fill with cottage cheese, jam, fruit, or ice cream; roll up and sprinkle with sugar and cinnamon. Lobster or crab newburg also makes a good filling (hot). These are suitable for any meal—breakfast, lunch, or dinner—depending on what you put in them. **Serves: 4**

PEABODY CONSERVATORY OF MUSIC

# Carrot Pudding

3 eggs
3 cups carrots, grated
2 cups light cream
¼ cup flour
1 teaspoon salt
¼ teaspoon pepper
½ teaspoon mace
4 tablespoons butter, melted

Preheat oven to 325° F. Beat eggs until frothy. Stir in carrots. Mix together flour, salt, pepper, and mace. Stir into egg mixture. Add melted butter and cream and stir for 3 minutes. Pour into buttered casserole and set in pan of boiling water. Add more water if necessary during cooking to keep water about 1″ up sides of casserole. Bake approximately 1½-2 hours. Pudding is done when a knife inserted in the center comes out clean. If there is custard sticking to it, it isn't done yet. **Serves: 4**

BOSTON COLLEGE

# Egg and Potato Casserole

mashed potatoes, seasoned
hard-cooked eggs, sliced
onions, sliced and in rings
American cheese, grated
butter
paprika, salt, pepper
minced parsley

Preheat oven to 400° F. Quantity depends on size of baking dish and how many you want to make this for. In a buttered pie plate, layer ingredients in this order: potatoes, eggs, onions, cheese. End up with a layer of potatoes and dot with butter and paprika, salt, and pepper to taste. Bake in oven 30 minutes. Sprinkle parsley over casserole just before serving. It looks interesting. Serve in pie plate. Then take out each portion. **Serves: Depends on quantity**

## ___ION COLLEGE

# Eggs Richard

6 slices bread, fresh or stale
6 slices Swiss cheese
6 eggs
butter
nutmeg
salt and pepper to taste

Preheat oven to 400° F. Cut crusts off bread. Fry one side only in butter until brown. Put slices of fried bread flat in greased baking dish or cookie sheet. Lay a slice of cheese on each slice of bread. Break an egg onto cheese. Some of the white will run over but the yolk should stay on. You can press down a little in the middle of the cheese, if necessary. Sprinkle with salt, pepper, and nutmeg, and bake until eggs are done. **Serves: 3**

## HOBART COLLEGE

# Lesley's Cheese Soufflé

*Not so difficult as most soufflés because it doesn't collapse easily. Prepare the day before.*

12 slices white bread
½ cup butter, softened
1 pound sharp cheddar cheese, grated
¼ cup melted butter
2 cups milk
1 teaspoon salt
1 teaspoon dry mustard
¼ teaspoon pepper
4 eggs

Preheat oven to 300° F. Remove crusts from bread and butter well. Cube. Put bread and grated cheese alternately in greased baking dish. Beat remaining ingredients with egg beater (not electric) and pour on bread and cheese. Place in refrigerator for at least 24 hours. Remove 1 hour before baking. If in a glass dish, bake 1 hour at 300° F—metal dish 1 hour at 325° F. **Serves: 4**

UPSALA COLLEGE, WIRTHS CAMPUS

# Cheese and Shrimp Soufflé

*This is a showstopper! Sure to please even the gourmet—and so easy!*

12 slices white bread
¼ pound butter, softened
1 pound small cooked shrimp
1¼ pound mild cheddar cheese, grated
6 eggs, beaten
3¼ cups milk
½ teaspoon salt
½ teaspoon paprika

Preheat oven to 350° F. Cut off bread crusts, butter bread, and cut into cubes. Grease 2½-quart casserole. Put in alternate layers of bread, shrimp and cheese, starting with bread and ending with cheese. Combine eggs, milk, and salt and pour into casserole (liquid should come to the last layer). Sprinkle with paprika. Refrigerate at least 6 hours or overnight. Bake for about 1 hour until puffy and brown. **Serves: 8**

UNIVERSITY OF NEW HAMPSHIRE

# The Whatever-You-Have-in-the-Fridge Quiche

1 unbaked pie crust
2 cups light cream, half & half, or milk
4 eggs
1-inch block Swiss cheese, cubed
¼-½ cup raw vegetables, steamed, or cooked
    vegetables reheated
2-3 tablespoons onions or scallions, thinly
    sliced
salt, pepper, and any other seasoning to taste

Preheat oven to 400° F. Prick pie crust sides and bottom with fork. Bake for 10 minutes. Set aside and lower oven to 350° F. In blender, blend cream or milk, scallion or onion, spices and eggs, added one at a time. Put vegetables into cooled pie crust. Top with cheese. Pour over liquid. Bake at 350° F for about 30 minutes or until knife inserted in middle comes out clean (moisture okay). **Serves: 4**

UNIVERSITY OF CALIFORNIA AT DAVIS

# California Omelet

4 eggs
2 tablespoons powdered sugar
2 oranges
½ tablespoon butter
2 tablespoons orange juice
3 tablespoons Grand Marnier (optional)
pinch salt

Peel oranges, divide into sections, and sprinkle with 2 tablespoons Grand Marnier and 1 tablespoon powdered sugar. Toss to mix and set aside. Break eggs into two bowls, separating yolks and whites. Combine yolks with orange juice and salt and beat until lemon-colored. Whip whites until stiff and fold into yolks. Fold in ½ of the orange sections. Heat omelet pan, add butter and swirl around to coat part way up the sides. When butter bubbles and starts to subside, pour in egg mixture. Lower heat and cook slowly. When bottom is lightly brown, add remaining orange sections, sprinkle with remaining sugar and Grand Marnier and put under broiler briefly until eggs are set and golden. **Serves: 2**

GEORGETOWN UNIVERSITY

# Baked Eggs in Cream

eggs (as many as you need—2 per person)
1½ teaspoons heavy cream per egg
2 tablespoons bread crumbs per egg
¼ teaspoon salt per egg
freshly grated nutmeg

Preheat oven to 350° F. Butter a baking dish big enough for the number of eggs you want to lie flat in one layer. Combine cream, crumbs, and salt. Line the bottom of the baking dish with one half the crumb mixture. Break eggs into saucer and slip, one at a time, into baking dish. Be careful not to break the yolks. Cover with remaining crumb mixture and sprinkle with freshly grated nutmeg. Bake until whites are firm and yolks are hot, about 10 minutes. **Serves: Depends on quantity**

# Notes & Recipes

# GROUND BEEF

**Recipes included and the chief ingredients needed.**

### FAIRLY CHEAP CHILI
Ground beef, pinto beans or canned kidney beans, tomato sauce, enchilada sauce, onions

### MEAT LOAF
Ground beef, onions, eggs, ketchup

### COCIDO
Ground beef, potatoes, green beans, chick peas, sausage

### HAMBURGERS HAWAIIAN
Ground beef, onions, eggs, ketchup

### MIKE'S CHILI
Ground beef, kidney beans, onions, green peppers, tomato paste, canned tomatoes

### STUFFED PEPPERS
Ground beef, onion, mushrooms, rice, tomato sauce, green peppers, cheddar cheese

### PEPPER BALLIES
Homemade or canned chili, onions, cheddar cheese, corn chips

### SHARI'S GRINDERS
Ground beef, egg, onions, Parmesan cheese, bread crumbs, Italian sausage, tomato sauce, green peppers

### CHINESE PEPPER GROUND STEAK
Ground beef, tomatoes, green peppers, ginger, cornstarch

### SPOONBURGERS
Ground beef, onions, green pepper, rice

### SWEET-SOUR MEATBALLS
Ground beef, pineapple chunks, brown sugar, cornstarch, water chestnuts, green pepper

### ENCHILADA CASSEROLE
Ground beef, flour, enchilada sauce, olives, tortillas, onions, grated cheese

### TASTY BURGERS
Ground beef, brown sugar, onions, chili sauce, celery

### BEEF STROGANOFF
Ground beef, garlic, onions, paprika, mushrooms, sour cream

### BEEF AND PINTO BEANS
Ground beef, pinto beans, tomato sauce, onion

### ZUCCHINI DINNER IN A DISH
Ground beef, zucchini, canned tomatoes, onion

### CHEESEBURGER CASSEROLE
Ground beef, onion, American cheese, broad noodles, canned tomatoes

### DANISH BARBECUE HAMBURGERS
Ground beef, beer, Worcestershire sauce, vinegar

# GROUND BEEF

### RED BEANS, RICE, AND BEEF
Ground beef, onions, kidney beans, stewed tomatoes, sherry

### TACOS
Ground beef, taco shells, onion, tomato sauce, cheddar cheese

### HAMBURGER NOODLE CASSEROLE
Ground beef, onions, noodles, cottage cheese, sour cream

Hamburger (or ground beef) is comparatively cheap, so you can eat it often. But it is so versatile there is no reason it should ever be boring. It has another big advantage over other inexpensive cuts of meat. It can be cooked quickly without the long hours of braising that are needed to make most cheap cuts tender. Another virtue of hamburger is the way it can be stretched. Less meat and more vegetables or pasta can be a boon when cash runs low or there are more than expected to dinner. Cook it as if you care, and you will dine well no matter how thriftily.

UNIVERSITY OF NEW HAMPSHIRE

# Fairly Cheap Chili

*Lasts a long time and it's hot because we like it that way. Great stuff! It's fairly cheap because you can use less meat and more beans without it making all that much difference.*

1 pound pinto beans or 2 cans kidney beans
2 pounds ground chuck
1 8-ounce can tomato sauce
2 10-ounce cans hot enchilada sauce
4 or more teaspoons chili powder
5-6 small onions, chopped

Boil pinto beans in 8 cups water until tender (takes time!). You will probably have to add more water before they are done. Sauté chuck and onions, drain fat before adding to drained cooked beans. Add sauce and chili powder and stir all together. Simmer for as long as you like. **Serves: 6-8**

VASSAR COLLEGE

# Meat Loaf

*Lots of people don't like meat loaf but we do because it's tasty, easy to make, and good cold in sandwiches.*

1 cup water with 1 bouillon cube dissolved
3 small onions, chopped
2 pounds ground beef
2 eggs, beaten
¼-½ cup ketchup
1½ cups soft bread crumbs
¾ cup warm water
salt and pepper to taste

Preheat oven to 350° F. Brown onions in a little oil. Add water and bouillon cube and simmer 5 minutes. Mix together in a bowl with all other ingredients. Salt and pepper to taste. Mix thoroughly. Shape into a loaf and place in loaf pan or shallow baking dish. Bake 1 hour. **Serves: 4-6**

NEW YORK UNIVERSITY
# Cocido

*This is what Spanish peasants often eat. Serve with hard crust bread, wine, and a green salad.*

> 2 quarts boiling water
> 6 potatoes, peeled and cut in quarters
> 1 pound green beans, cut in 1″ pieces
> 1 can chick peas, drained
> 1 pound chopped round steak or chopped stew meat
> ½ pound spicy sausage, sliced
> 1 garlic clove, minced
> 1 onion, chopped
> 1 teaspoon mint (or several minced fresh sprigs)
> 1 bouillon cube
> salt and pepper to taste

Add potatoes and green beans to 2 quarts boiling salted water and simmer 25 minutes. Add chick peas last 5 minutes. While vegetables are cooking, brown chopped meat with garlic and onion. Remove meat, drain pan, and fry sliced sausages 8 minutes. Drain fat, add chopped meat and sausage to vegetables when vegetables are tender. Simmer 10 minutes. Serve in two courses.

Soup is the liquid drained off the meat and vegetables plus one bouillon cube and seasoning to taste. You can add a cupful of cooked rice or any pasta if you like. Main course is meat and vegetables. You can serve each ingredient piled separately on the plate or all together. If you wish to serve them separately (and that means cooking them separately), you have to use a lot more pots. To make more or less than this recipe, keep proportions roughly equal except for less sausage (proportionately). **Serves: 6-8**

UNIVERSITY OF LOUISVILLE
# Hamburgers Hawaiian

> 1 pound ground beef
> 1 medium onion, minced
> 1 clove garlic, minced
> ½ cup soy sauce
> ¼ teaspoon ginger

Mix beef and onion and shape into 8 patties. Put in shallow baking dish. Combine remaining ingredients and pour over patties. Let stand 30 minutes, turning once. Drain and broil or pan-fry. Serve with sliced pineapple. **Serves: 4**

SCHOOL OF THE MUSEUM OF FINE ARTS

# Mike's Chili

*If you buy chili in cans, it's almost all beans. This is better and cheaper, and you can make extra to keep in the refrigerator and heat up when someone is hungry.*

   2 pounds ground beef
   2-3 medium onions, chopped
   2 cans kidney beans, drained
   1 green pepper, chopped (optional)
   1 teaspoon tomato paste
   2 1-pound cans whole tomatoes
   2 teaspoons chili powder
   salt and pepper to taste

Brown meat and onions in skillet. Drain fat. Add kidney beans, green pepper, tomato paste, tomatoes, and seasonings. Simmer covered about 30 minutes—longer if time is available. **Serves: 4-6**

SCHOOL OF THE MUSEUM OF FINE ARTS

# Stuffed Peppers

   1 pound ground beef
   1 onion, chopped
   1 pound mushrooms, sliced
   1 cup cooked rice
   2 cups tomato sauce
   3 green peppers, cut in half and seeded
   cheddar cheese, grated

Preheat oven to 325° F. Mix first five ingredients together and stuff into peppers. Set upright in pan and bake 30-45 minutes. Last 5 minutes, take out and dot with cheddar cheese. Stick back in oven until cheese melts. **Serves: 3**

UNIVERSITY OF DENVER

# Pepper Ballies

*This is a favorite at the Antelope Valley Fair in Lancaster, California, every September.*

   1 can chili (or your own)
   ½ pound cheddar cheese, grated
   1 onion, chopped
   corn chips

Heat chili until very hot. Grate cheese. Chop onion. In individual bowls, put a layer of chips. Spoon chili over these. Cover with a layer of cheese (it'll melt). Add onion to taste. We serve this with red wine and a loaf of bread with the rest of the cheese melted on top. **Serves: 2**

UNIVERSITY OF BRIDGEPORT

# Shari's Grinders

**Meatballs:**

½ pound ground beef
1 egg
1 onion, minced
2 teaspoons garlic salt
3 tablespoons parsley flakes
½ cup Parmesan cheese, grated
1 cup bread crumbs
salt and pepper to taste

Mix all ingredients together and shape into balls.

½ pound Italian sausage (sweet and hot,
    mixed), sliced
3 cans tomato sauce
4 large green peppers, cut in narrow strips
2 medium onions, cut in narrow strips
2-3 tablespoons salad oil

Brown meatballs and sausages. Drain fat. Remove from pan. Sauté onions and pepper in oil until soft. Add meat mixture and tomato sauce and simmer 30 minutes covered, stirring once or twice. Spoon into grinders or pita bread. **Serves: 4**

RICE UNIVERSITY

# Chinese Pepper Ground Steak

*You can make this with sliced steak, but this way we can afford to have it more often and it tastes just as good.*

1½ pounds ground beef
1 garlic clove, minced
3 tomatoes, chopped
4 green peppers, seeded and cut into strips
¼ cup soy sauce
¼ teaspoon pepper
½ teaspoon sugar
1½ teaspoons ginger
1¼ cups hot water with bouillon cube
2 tablespoons cornstarch

Shape meat into small patties and brown with garlic. Drain fat. Add tomatoes and green peppers. Add seasonings and all liquids except ½ cup beef bouillon mixture. Cover and cook for 20 minutes. Mix cornstarch with remaining beef stock and stir into meat mixture. Simmer for a few minutes until thickened, stirring constantly. Serve with hot rice. **Serves: 4-6**

ɪᴀ Uɴɪᴠᴇʀsɪᴛʏ

# Spoonburgers

1 pound ground beef
2 onions, sliced
1 green pepper, chopped
½ cup chicken broth
¼ cup cooked rice
¼ teaspoon dry mustard
2 tablespoons ketchup
salt and pepper to taste

Brown beef and onion in frying pan. Drain fat. Add peppers and cook 3 more minutes. Mix broth, rice, mustard, ketchup. Pour over mixture of meat and onions and peppers. Simmer 10 minutes and serve over rice, toast, or hot dog roll. **Serves: 4**

Nᴇᴡ Eɴɢʟᴀɴᴅ Cᴏɴsᴇʀᴠᴀᴛᴏʀʏ ᴏғ Mᴜsɪᴄ

# Sweet-Sour Meatballs

*These should be served with hot, cooked rice—so make some along with the rest of the recipe.*

1 pound ground beef
1 cup bread crumbs
1 bouillon cube
1 cup pineapple chunks
¼ cup brown sugar, packed
3 tablespoons cornstarch
¼ cup cider vinegar
1 teaspoon soy sauce
1 5-ounce can water chestnuts, drained and thinly sliced
1 green pepper, cut in strips

Mix meat and bread crumbs with salt and pepper as you like it, and form into medium-sized meatballs. Sauté until well browned on all sides. Drain fat. Add ½ cup hot water and bouillon cube. Cover and simmer 30 minutes. Drain pineapple, reserving syrup. In medium saucepan, combine brown sugar and cornstarch. Blend in pineapple syrup, ½ cup water, vinegar, and soy sauce. Cook and stir over low heat until mixture thickens. Gradually stir in meatballs, with their pan gravy, water chestnuts, green pepper, and pineapple. Heat to boiling. Serve over rice. Garnish with tomatoes. **Serves: 4**

UNIVERSITY OF NEW HAMPSHIRE

# Enchilada Casserole

*This one is great!*

2 pounds ground beef
3 tablespoons chili powder
1½ teaspoons salt
oregano
½ cup flour (or less)
2 small cans enchilada sauce
½ cup water
2 cups sliced olives
2 dozen tortillas (approximately)
grated cheese
chopped onions

Brown meat. Drain fat. Add chili powder, salt, oregano, and flour. Go easy on the flour. See how thick you like it (it thickens as it cooks). Add liquids and simmer 10 minutes. Add olives, reserving a few. Simmer 2-3 minutes more. In large greased casserole, place layer of meat mixture with *quartered* tortillas. Add ½ of remaining meat mixture and generous amounts of cheese and onion. Then another layer of tortillas and remaining sauce. Finish with cheese and onions and rest of sauce. Bake for 30 minutes. This freezes well. **Serves: 4**

UNIVERSITY OF LOUISVILLE

# Tasty Burgers

1 pound ground beef
1 tablespoon brown sugar
2 tablespoons onion, diced
2 tablespoons celery, diced
¾ cup chili sauce
1 teaspoon prepared mustard
1 tablespoon vinegar
½ teaspoon salt

Brown meat. Drain fat. Add rest of ingredients and simmer until done. Spoon onto warm hamburger buns and serve. **Serves: 3-4**

VASSAR COLLEGE

# Beef Stroganoff

1½ pounds ground beef
½ cup onions, sliced
1 clove garlic on toothpick
2 tablespoons flour
1 pound fresh mushrooms, sliced
1 cup chicken broth
1 cup sour cream
2 teaspoons salt
¼ teaspoon pepper
dash paprika

Brown beef and onions with garlic. Drain fat. Sprinkle with flour and toss in frying pan. Add seasoning and rest of ingredients. Heat thoroughly, stirring frequently. Serve over hot rice. **Serves: 6-8**

UNIVERSITY OF PITTSBURGH

# Beef and Pinto Beans

1½ cups pinto beans
1 onion, chopped
2 cups hot tomato sauce with chili powder to
    taste
1 pound ground beef

Cook pinto beans until soft. Mush them up (we use our hands) add some of the chopped onion and sauce and refry for awhile—about 10 minutes. Brown hamburger with the rest of the onions. Drain fat. Add hot sauce. Serve beans and hamburger with fresh tomatoes and shredded lettuce. You can serve with taco or burrito shells (fried in oil) and piled all together with a side dish of guacamole. It's a good meal, especially with cold beer. If you like it really hot, add a few hot peppers in the cooking. **Serves: 3-4**

WILLIAM SMITH COLLEGE
# Zucchini Dinner in a Dish

*There is only one pot to wash for a really good dinner.*

- 1 cup onion, chopped
- 2 pounds ground beef
- 3 medium-sized zucchini, sliced
- 2 cans whole tomatoes
- 2 tablespoons Parmesan cheese, grated
- 1 clove garlic, minced

Brown onions and meat together. Drain fat. Add remaining ingredients. Cook at medium-low heat for 45 minutes on top of stove. Salt and pepper to taste. Serve sprinkled with grated Parmesan cheese. **Serves: 6-8**

SCHOOL OF THE MUSEUM OF FINE ARTS
# Cheeseburger Casserole

- 1 pound ground beef
- 1 onion, grated
- 1½ cups broad noodles, cooked
- 1 can tomatoes without juice (optional)
- 1 cup American cheese, diced

Crumble hamburger and onion in skillet, and brown. Drain fat. Add drained hot noodles and toss. Add tomatoes. Stir in cheese. Cook about 10 minutes or until cheese bubbles.

**Variation**: Also good with leftover ham and diced pineapple. Omit cheese and tomato and use ½ cup pineapple juice. **Serves: 4-6**

# Danish Barbecue Hamburgers

½ cup beer
2 pounds ground beef, shaped into patties
½ cup ketchup
2 tablespoons Worcestershire sauce
2 tablespoons vinegar
½ teaspoon salt
¼ teaspoon pepper

Pour out beer and let stand at least 15 minutes before using. Meanwhile, brown hamburger in frying pan. Drain fat. Mix together beer and all other ingredients. Pour over hamburger and let simmer for 10 minutes or until hamburger is done. **Serves: 4-6**

# Red Beans, Rice, and Beef

*This recipe can be made with one hot plate and one electric (or nonelectric) frypan in 30 minutes (with practice).*

¾ pound ground beef
1-2 white onions, chopped
½ teaspoon thyme ⎤ or whatever seasonings
½ teaspoon marjoram ⎦ you prefer
chili powder (start with a teaspoon and work up to your taste)
1 large can kidney beans (1-1½ pounds, depending on how far meat has to be stretched)
1 large can stewed tomatoes (can also use tomato puree, which will make a thicker sauce)
sherry to taste (optional)

Fry beef, onions, and seasoning until meat is brown and onions are clear. Drain fat. Add kidney beans and tomatoes. I mix this with my hands, but you can use a bowl and a spoon. Simmer for however long you have—at least 20 minutes. Serve over hot rice. **Serves: 4**

**Note**: Most stores, from time to time, sell day-old mushrooms at *very* low prices. These can be sautéed with onions and meat (omit chili powder) for an entirely different dish. The mushrooms are good (if you like mushrooms) in almost anything—except they're really a little far "gone" for a salad.

UNIVERSITY OF CALIFORNIA AT LOS ANGELES

# Tacos

*These are taco shells (tortillas fried in oil and folded in half) with meat filling.*

6 taco shells
1 pound ground beef
1 large onion, diced
1 cup hot sauce (tomato sauce heated with
    chili powder or canned
    chili sauce)
½ cup cheddar cheese, grated
salt and pepper to taste

Prepare taco shells by frying tortillas in oil and folding in half. Brown meat and onions. Drain fat. Spoon into folded tacos, cover with sauce, sprinkle with grated cheese. Serve with shredded lettuce, tomato salad, and a bottle of Tabasco® for those who like it hotter than you made it. **Serves: 3**

VASSAR COLLEGE

# Hamburger Noodle Casserole

8 ounces noodles, cooked
1 pound ground beef
1 medium onion, chopped
1 pound cottage cheese
1 pint sour cream
grated Parmesan cheese
salt and pepper to taste

Preheat oven to 300° F. Cook noodles and drain. Keep hot. Grease casserole baking dish and set aside. Brown hamburger in skillet. Add onion and seasoning, and cook until onion is tender. Drain fat from meat mixture and combine in casserole with noodles, cottage cheese, and sour cream. Cover with Parmesan cheese (sprinkled over top as thickly as you like) and bake for 30 minutes. **Serves: 4**

# BEEF

**Recipes included and the chief ingredients needed.**

SWEDISH CASSEROLE
Stew beef, cabbage, turnips, molasses

SHISH KEBAB WITHOUT THE KEBAB
Stew beef, green peppers, tomatoes, onions,
barbecue sauce

DIGGER'S DELIGHT
Stew beef, onions, carrots, turnip, potatoes, flour

BRAZILIAN BEEF CASSEROLE
Stew beef, potatoes, celery, green pepper, coffee,
wine

SCANDINAVIAN BEEF LIVER
Beef liver, prunes, apples, milk

SUSANNAH'S BEEF STEW
Stew beef, carrots, celery, potatoes, tomato sauce
or tomatoes

# BEEF

Meat is an excellent source of complete protein—unfortunately, it is also the most expensive. However, since the cheapest cuts are just as good, sometimes even better for you than the most expensive, patience and cooking skill really pay off. Most inexpensive cuts of beef require longer, slower cooking, but their flavor is as good as the costliest cuts and they lend themselves to a lot more variety. The longer cooking time isn't really an inconvenience because it doesn't mean hanging around and watching it. Once it is in the oven or on the stove simmering away, you can forget about it until it is ready.

TEXAS CHRISTIAN UNIVERSITY

# Swedish Casserole

2 pounds stew beef or some inexpensive cut,
  cut in chunks
1 medium cabbage, coarsely chopped
2 turnips, sliced
2 tablespoons molasses
¼ teaspoon marjoram
2 tablespoons caraway seeds
2 teaspoons salt
2 cups hot water

Preheat oven to 350° F. Turn everything into a casserole or skillet and either bake in the oven or simmer slowly on top of stove for 1 ½ hours. Serve with mashed potatoes. **Serves: 4**

UNION COLLEGE, SCHENECTADY, NY

# Shish Kebab without the Kebab

*This is fast, easy, and delicious. We like to serve it with yellow curried rice. (See page 106.) It feeds a mob but you can cut it down as much as you like.*

6 green peppers
6 tomatoes
6 medium-small onions
5 pounds stew beef, cut in chunks
4 jars barbecue sauce with mushrooms (or
  make your own)

Cut peppers, tomatoes, and onions into eighths. Put in large bowl or bowls and add meat and sauce. Toss until everything is completely coated with sauce. Marinate for 3 hours (or more, if convenient—even overnight is okay in the refrigerator). Line cake pan with foil, place meat and vegetables in rows in pan as if on a skewer but without the skewer. Pour on marinade liquid from bowls. Broil, turning once, approximately 15 minutes. Test for doneness by cutting into one piece of meat. **Serves: 15-20**

UNIVERSITY OF TEXAS
# Digger's Delight

*An authentic Australian stew that requires one to first catch and skin a kangaroo. If such an animal is not readily available (local zoos are touchy), then be guided by the following:*

1½ pounds stew beef
3 medium onions
6 medium carrots
1 turnip
2 large potatoes
2 tablespoons oil
¼ cup flour
1 teaspoon salt
¼ teaspoon pepper

Cut beef to bite size and dredge in flour. Heat oil in pot and drop in meat. Brown on all sides. Pour off oil. Add 2 cups water and bring to boil. Prepare vegetables to bite size. Add to meat. Add salt and pepper. Cover and cook on low heat approximately 2-3 hours at just simmering.

Bisquick® dumplings are a good addition. Just 1 cup of Bisquick® mixed with approximately ⅓ cup of milk (needs to be on dry side—disregard package instructions). Roll in ball and break off into 7 or 8 small balls. Twenty minutes before serving time place dumplings gently on top of stew. Cook for 10 minutes with lid off, then another 10 minutes covered. Dig in and eat hearty. **Serves: 3-4**

BOSTON UNIVERSITY
# Brazilian Beef Casserole

*If you don't want to simmer this on top of the stove, it can just as easily be done in the oven. Cover and don't let cook above simmer.*

2 pounds stew beef, cut in chunks
4 potatoes, quartered
2 stalks celery, sliced
1 green pepper, chopped
1 cup strong coffee
1 clove
1 teaspoon cinnamon
¾ cup sweet or dry wine to taste (optional)
¼ cup flour

Brown meat in a little butter. Add all other ingredients, except flour, and simmer approximately 45 minutes to 1 ½ hours, or until meat is tender. Sprinkle flour gradually into stew, stirring constantly. Or mix small amount of sauce with flour in separate bowl, then add to pot. Cook, stirring, until slightly thickened. **Serves: 4**

BOSTON COLLEGE

# Scandinavian Beef Liver

*This is great for people who think they don't like liver.*

6 slices beef liver
2 cups cooked prunes, pitted and chopped
8 apples, peeled, cored, sliced
milk
salt and pepper to taste

Preheat oven to 350° F. Butter casserole. Wash liver, remove outside skin and membranes. Slices must be uniform and large enough to roll. Don't settle for bits and pieces or ends. Lay liver slices flat on wax paper and almost cover with prunes and apples. Roll slices up with prunes and apples (like a jelly roll) and skewer with toothpicks. Lay in casserole and pour in milk until it just covers the meat. Bake until milk is absorbed and completely disappears. Very good served with yams. **Serves: 4-6**

VASSAR COLLEGE

# Susannah's Beef Stew

2½ pounds beef stew chunks
7 carrots, sliced
4 stalks celery, sliced
6 potatoes, quartered
2 beef bouillon cubes, dissolved in 2 cups boiling water
1 large can tomato sauce or tomatoes (tomatoes will make it thinner)
1 bay leaf
salt and pepper to taste

Place everything in casserole, cover and bake for 2½-3 hours. If you use tomato sauce, you may need to add a little more liquid. Since this tastes even better the second or third day, we sometimes make it ahead. It is easily heated up and makes a great leftover. **Serves: 5-6**

# Notes & Recipes

# CHICKEN

**Recipes included and the chief ingredients needed.**

CHARLES'S CHICKEN VERONIQUE
Broilers, broth, white wine, white grapes

CHICKEN AND OLIVES
Fryer, canned tomatoes, olives, wine

PAM'S CHICKEN AND MUSHROOMS
Broiler, eggs, milk, bread crumbs, mozzarella
cheese, mushrooms

ELAINE'S CHICKEN CACCIATORE
Broiler or fryer, spaghetti sauce, stuffed Spanish
olives, tomato sauce, wine

CAROL'S BARBECUED CHICKEN
Broiler or fryer, peach preserves

MARINATED CHICKEN
Chicken, olive oil, spices

CHARLIE'S CHICKEN CORDON BLEU
Chicken breasts, sliced ham, cheddar cheese,
Swiss cheese, bread crumbs

CHICKEN LIVERS AND TOMATOES
Chicken livers, onions, tomatoes, soy sauce

NORALYN'S CHICKEN
Broiler, soy sauce, peanut oil, spices

GARLIC CHICKEN
Broiler, garlic

ELLEN'S SESAME CHICKEN
Broiler or fryer, sesame seeds, white wine

EASY CHICKEN CURRY
Broiler or fryer, curry powder

NEW ORLEANS CHICKEN
Fryer, canned tomatoes, onion, celery, green
pepper

MABLE DESMOND'S CHICKEN
Broiler or fryer, onions

PINEAPPLE CHICKEN
Chicken breasts, cooked rice, pineapple chunks,
raisins

CHICKEN SUPREME IN MAGIC
MUSHROOM SAUCE
Chicken breasts, flour, mushrooms, onions,
tarragon, chicken broth, sour cream, cognac

ERIC'S CHICKEN AND TOMATOES
Broiler or fryer, stewed tomatoes, onion

# CHICKEN

Chicken is so inexpensive you can afford to eat it often. It lends itself to a wide variety of dishes—from bland to hot—and is the most versatile of all leftovers. All poultry is very perishable and should be refrigerated promptly even when cooked. If you have a large amount of chicken in a pot of broth or soup, take out all the chicken and other solids, put in a tightly covered container and refrigerate. Put the pan of broth in cold water (in the sink is okay) and keep the water cold by changing when necessary. Do this for about 15 minutes and then refrigerate. **Never** just let it stand on a counter or stove until it cools off.

If you are planning to roast a stuffed turkey, do not stuff it until just before you put it in the oven. You can make the stuffing the day before, but don't put it inside the turkey. **Never, never** stuff it the day before.

Chicken comes in many different forms and you need to know the differences if you are to buy wisely.

**Broilers**. Small, tender chickens, usually under three pounds. Good for broiling, all right for roasting whole. Chicken parts are usually cut-up broilers or fryers and are a very expensive way to buy chicken. However, if you want just boned chicken breasts for a particular recipe, bone them yourself and save a lot of money. It is very easy. Ask your butcher to show you, get a book out of the library, or just buy a good boning knife and try to cut the meat off the bones by running the knife right along the bone, separating the bone from the meat as you do so. The boning knife pays for itself the first time you use it.

**Fryers**. Just like broilers only somewhat bigger. They stand up better for frying because they don't dry out so quickly. Fine for broiling, too. Also good for all casserole dishes.

**Roasting chickens and capons**. Good for roast chicken or casseroles.

**Hen, fowl, stewing chickens**. Best for soup, boiled chicken, etc. If you try to make soup from a broiler, it won't have much flavor. (If this happens, cheat a little and add a chicken bouillon cube.) A really nice 5-6 pound fowl cooked for 3 or 4 hours is your best bet for soup or stock.

**Caution**: All chickens (except parts) come with giblets, which are heart, liver, gizzard, and neck. Hunt for them. In a roasting chicken, they will be found packed inside somewhere; sometimes in the neck cavity, sometimes in the other end. If you absentmindedly roast the chicken without removing the giblets and the paper they are wrapped in, the results may be inedible. Take them out and save them for making giblet gravy or giblet stew or to enrich chicken stock.

**To roast poultry in foil**. Turn oven 25° F higher than your recipe calls for. Open up the foil during the last third of your cooking time and baste occasionally to brown. For safety's sake, though, put the foil-wrapped package in a pan. Otherwise you may spill the drippings when you lift the foil from the oven at the end of cooking.

UNIVERSITY OF VERMONT

## Charles's Chicken Veronique

*Very good with tossed salad and rice (or noodles).*

2 broilers, cut up
¼ cup salad oil
1 teaspoon salt
1 teaspoon rosemary
¼ teaspoon black pepper
¼ teaspoon thyme
1 garlic clove, minced
1 bay leaf
1½ cups chicken broth
¼ cup milk or cream
1 tablespoon cornstarch
½ cup white wine (optional)
3 cups white grapes (can be canned)

Brown chicken in hot oil in skillet. Remove pieces as they brown. Drain leftover oil and add chicken broth to skillet. Stir in salt, rosemary, pepper, thyme, garlic, and bay leaf. Mix 1 tablespoon of cornstarch with milk or cream and stir it into broth until broth thickens. Add chicken and simmer covered for 40 minutes. Add more broth if sauce gets too thick, but remember to allow for the wine. When ready to serve, add wine and grapes and just heat through. **Serves: 6-8**

UNIVERSITY OF DENVER

## Chicken and Olives

*Great if you like olives as much as we do.*

1 fryer, cut up
¼ cup olive oil
1 can tomatoes or 1 ½ cups chopped fresh
    tomatoes
1 garlic clove, minced
1 can pitted black olives or 1 bottle stuffed
    olives
2-3 tablespoons sherry, Chablis, or sauterne
    (optional)

Brown fryer in olive oil. Add tomatoes, garlic, olives, and wine. Cover and simmer for 30 minutes. **Serves: 2-4**

UNIVERSITY OF VERMONT

# Pam's Chicken and Mushrooms

*A really good recipe for chicken.*

Preheat oven to 475° F. Bone a broiler (cheaper than buying it cut up and it only takes a minute!). Pound pieces flat. Make a batter of 2 eggs and 1 cup of milk, beaten together. Dip chicken in egg mixture, then in bread crumbs. Fry in hot butter until golden brown—about 15 minutes. Put browned chicken in greased baking dish. Top with mozzarella cheese and sautéed mushrooms (or canned button mushrooms, sliced and heated). Top with buttered bread crumbs. Place in oven and bake until cheese is melted and bread crumbs are golden brown.

BOSTON COLLEGE

# Elaine's Chicken Cacciatore

*My special creation that takes almost no time to prepare is inexpensive, tastes delicious!*

1 fryer or broiler, cut in pieces
¼ cup olive oil
1 clove garlic, minced
1 medium jar spaghetti sauce
1 large can tomato sauce
1 small jar stuffed Spanish olives
½ teaspoon oregano
½ teaspoon basil
1 teaspoon onion salt
10 ounces inexpensive Chianti wine (optional)

Preheat oven to 350° F. Salt and pepper chicken and saute in olive oil and garlic until golden brown. When well browned, remove and keep hot in baking dish. While chicken is sautéing, put spaghetti sauce, tomato sauce, olives (and olive juice), spices, and wine in saucepan. Heat to simmering and pour over chicken. Bake for 25 minutes.

I often use this as a side dish with spaghetti. If you can afford it, serve as a main dish with the spaghetti on the side. The sauce can be stretched to accommodate as much spaghetti as you need for unexpected company by adding more Chianti and a small can of tomato paste.
**Serves: 4-6**

BOSTON UNIVERSITY

# Carol's Barbecued Chicken

*This is great!*

1 broiler or fryer, cut up
¼ cup melted butter (you may need more)
½ teaspoon barbecue sauce (bottled is fine)
½ teaspoon garlic salt
Secret Ingredient: 1 teaspoon peach preserves

Preheat oven to 350° F. Place chicken in shallow pan. Coat with sauce of all other ingredients mixed together well. Bake 45 minutes to 1 hour. If you like, turn on broiler and broil the last 10 minutes of cooking time to make browner. Be sure to spoon liquid in pan over chicken every 15 minutes or so. **Serves: 2-4**

NEW YORK UNIVERSITY

# Marinated Chicken

Make a marinade of olive oil, salt, pepper, and oregano. Put in pieces of chicken (a broiler cut up), and refrigerate for 1-2 hours, turning occasionally. Put chicken in 350° F oven for 30 minutes and baste with marinade as it is cooking. Pour pan juices over chicken when you serve it.

UNIVERSITY OF VERMONT

# Charlie's Chicken Cordon Bleu

*The more cheese the better. Just double ingredients to serve more. For a party, serve lots of rice.*

4 chicken breasts, boned
½ pound sliced ham, coarsely chopped
¼ pound cheddar cheese, shredded
½ pound Swiss cheese, shredded
1 cup bread crumbs
1 teaspoon tarragon
salt and pepper to taste
3 tablespoons butter

Preheat oven to 350° F. Pound chicken flat. On each breast place a layer of ham, then cheddar and Swiss cheese. Roll and secure with toothpicks. Place in buttered baking dish and dot with butter. Sprinkle with bread crumbs mixed with tarragon. Bake for 40 minutes. **Serves: 2-4**

# Chicken Livers and Tomatoes

1 pound chicken livers
2 small onions, thinly sliced
3 tablespoons butter
3 tomatoes, cut into small pieces
1 tablespoon vinegar
1 tablespoon soy sauce
salt and pepper to taste
½ teaspoon garlic (cumin, cloves, ginger, coriander, or curry powder can also be used)

Separate each liver into 2 pieces. (This is natural, as you will see when you look at the livers.) Slice onions thin and fry in butter until yellow. Add livers and sauté, stirring frequently. Add tomatoes. Add water if necessary to keep from burning. Add vinegar, soy sauce. Season as desired. Add enough water to keep some liquid in the pan, and simmer, covered for 8 minutes.

If you want to serve this over rice or spaghetti, make more sauce by adding more water and some tomato paste and you will have as much sauce as you need. You may have to add more seasoning; in this event, just taste as you go along. Substitute mushrooms for onions if your budget will stand it. **Serves: 2-3**

# Noralyn's Chicken

*This is an easy recipe for a party—just double or triple the ingredients. It's quick to make once the chicken is marinated. Even the rice can be made ahead of time and reheated.*

Cut up a broiler. Marinate 2-3 hours, or even overnight, in soy sauce, peanut oil, minced fresh ginger, minced garlic cloves, dry mustard, lemon juice, and a little salt. Drain chicken and broil as usual, brushing with the marinade a couple of times while cooking. Five minutes before chicken is ready, sprinkle with chopped peanuts. The marinade can be heated and served in a separate dish along with the juice in the broiling pan. Serve with a big bowl of rice. **Serves: 4-6**

# Garlic Chicken

*Chicken needs variations because we eat it so often. The memory of this one stays with you.*

Preheat oven to 350° F. Put a cut-up broiler in a shallow dish. Add a lot of butter (dotted all over) and minced garlic (lots—like two or more cloves). Cover with aluminum foil and bake for 1 hour. Uncover the last 15 minutes of cooking so it will brown.

UNIVERSITY OF PITTSBURGH

# Ellen's Sesame Chicken

1 broiler or fryer, cut up
1 cup buttered bread crumbs
1 cup white wine (optional)
½ teaspoon thyme
1 cup sesame seeds, toasted
salt and pepper to taste

Preheat oven to 400° F. Arrange broiler in shallow baking dish. Pour wine over chicken. Mix bread crumbs, sesame seeds, thyme, salt, and pepper. Sprinkle over top of chicken. Bake 1 hour.
   **Note**: Most sesame seeds are not toasted when you buy them. We toast a batch in the oven and keep them handy for cooking. **Serves: 2-4**

BARNARD COLLEGE

# Easy Chicken Curry

*This is a good recipe for other kinds of meat, too.*

1 broiler, or fryer, cut in pieces
½ cup butter, melted
1 teaspoon curry powder
salt and pepper to taste

Preheat oven to 400° F. Bake chicken seasoned with salt and pepper in oven or broiler/oven for 35 minutes, turning 2 or 3 times to brown evenly. Mix butter with curry and pour over chicken just before serving. Serve on bed of hot cooked rice.
**Serves: 2-4**

UNIVERSITY OF TEXAS

# New Orleans Chicken

1 fryer, cut up
1 cup flour
3 tablespoons butter
1 large onion, chopped
2 stalks celery, chopped
1 green pepper, chopped
1 can tomatoes
1 cup boiling water
1 teaspoon sugar
1 tablespoon Worcestershire sauce
salt and pepper to taste

Flour chicken and sauté until golden brown on all sides. Remove and keep hot. Put in onion, celery, and green pepper. Cook, stirring constantly, 5 minutes. Add tomatoes, boiling water, sugar, Worcestershire sauce, and seasonings. Simmer 5 minutes. Put chicken in sauce, cover, and let simmer 1 ¼ hours. Thicken gravy with cornstarch, if desired, and serve with rice.
**Serves: 2-4**

# Mable Desmond's Chicken

1 broiler or fryer, cut up
2 large onions, chopped
1 cup water
seasoned salt, enough to sprinkle over
    chicken

Preheat oven to 350° F. Place cut-up chicken pieces in a flat pan. Sprinkle with seasoned salt and onions. Pour water into one corner of pan (not over chicken or all the seasoning will be washed off). Cover with foil unless pan has its own cover. Simmer on top of stove 30 minutes (2 burners if large pan). Then put in oven for 1 hour, adding water if necessary (keep checking). Uncover last 15 minutes to brown. **Serves: 2-4**

# Pineapple Chicken

*A budget dish that makes a good one-dish company meal.*

2 cups cooked rice
pineapple chunks; reserve 1 cup juice
raisins
3-4 chicken breasts, cooked in chunks
butter
brown sugar
1 tablespoon soy sauce

Preheat oven to 350° F. Grease a deep casserole dish. Then layer with rice, pineapple chunks, raisins, and chicken. Dot with butter and sprinkle with brown sugar. Repeat layering until ingredients are used up. Mix pineapple juice with soy sauce and pour over layered ingredients. Bake until heated through—about 30 minutes.

What's good about this dish is you can use leftover rice or chicken. Be as skimpy with the chicken as you want to be. Can toss in nuts. **Serves: 3-4**

GEORGETOWN UNIVERSITY

# Chicken Supreme in Magic Mushroom Sauce

10 chicken breasts, skinned and boned
salt and pepper
flour
½ cup butter
½ pound fresh mushrooms, finely chopped
3 green onions, chopped
4 tablespoons flour
1 tablespoon tarragon
2 cups chicken broth
1 cup sour cream
3 tablespoons cognac (optional)
chopped parsley

Preheat oven to 325° F. Season breasts with salt and pepper and roll in flour. Sauté gently in ¼ cup butter until brown on all sides. Place chicken breasts in baking pan or casserole. Add remaining butter to skillet and add mushrooms. Sauté for 2 minutes. Add green onions. Sprinkle with flour, stirring to blend. Add tarragon and chicken broth. Cook, stirring continuously, until mixture boils. Remove from heat. Pour sauce over chicken breasts. Cover and bake at 325° F for 30 minutes. Remove chicken from casserole and keep hot in oven while you quickly add the sour cream and cognac to the sauce. Heat, stirring constantly. *Do not let boil.* Pour sauce into bowl. Put chicken back in casserole or pan and pour sauce over it. Reheat in oven if necessary but not to boiling. Sprinkle with parsley just before serving. **Serves: 6-8**

UNIVERSITY OF PITTSBURGH

# Eric's Chicken and Tomatoes

1 broiler or fryer, cut up
2 cans stewed tomatoes
2 small onions, minced
2 cups mushrooms, sliced (optional)
½ tablespoon marjoram *or* sage
3 tablespoons butter
1 cup sherry (optional)
salt and pepper to taste

Preheat oven to 400° F. Put chicken in casserole and dot with all the butter. Sprinkle with herbs, salt, and pepper. Bake 30 minutes, then add remaining ingredients and bake another 30 minutes. **Serves: 2-4**

# FISH

### Recipes included and the chief ingredients needed.

SHRIMP 'N' RICE
Shrimp, onion, safflower oil, garlic, sauterne

SHRIMP PILAU
Onion, cloves, cinnamon stick, cardamom seeds, chicken broth, turmeric, shrimp, raisins, cashews

FISH SCALLOP
Fish fillets, onion, Swiss cheese, sour cream, sherry, currants, walnuts

TUNA-VEGETABLE MIX
Canned tunafish, brown rice, peas, canned corn

BAKED STUFFED HADDOCK
Haddock fillets, sesame seeds, shrimp, butter, white wine

PATTY'S JAMBALAYA
Onion, hot sausage, tomato sauce, shrimp, garlic, green pepper, parsley

BAKED HERBED FISH
Fish fillets, spinach, almonds

TUNAFISH CASSEROLE
Canned tunafish, peas, onions, green peppers, lemon juice, white sauce, mushrooms, spaghetti, sherry

BAKED FLOUNDER IN SOUR CREAM
Fish fillets, sour cream, mushrooms, mayonnaise

SALMON AND MUSHROOM CASSEROLE
Canned salmon, brown rice, white sauce, cheddar cheese, raisins, broccoli, mushrooms

FISH FILLETS IN WHITE WINE
Fish fillets, lemon, white wine

# FISH

Fish is popular to eat but not to cook, according to many students. They find it is often impractical for the conditions under which they cook (in dorms, for instance), and they can't always find a good fish store or fish department where they market. They also think that fish isn't as flexible as meat; if plans change and it can't be cooked that evening as intended, they feel uneasy about keeping it for another night. Canned fish doesn't present the same problems, as I could see from the number of you who sent in practically the same recipes in this category.

University of Denver

# Shrimp 'n' Rice

*Here's my favorite—it takes only 20 minutes. The same recipe works for sole, haddock, or whatever fish you have.*

½ cup chopped onion
1 tablespoon safflower oil
1 garlic clove, minced
1 bay leaf, crushed
1 teaspoon minced parsley
1½ pounds shrimp (the frozen little ones do quite well)
1 cup sauterne wine (optional)
salt and pepper to taste
1 teaspoon cornstarch

Sauté onion in oil until the onion starts to color. Add garlic, bay leaf, parsley, and shrimp. Sauté 3 minutes. Add sauterne, salt, and pepper. Cover and simmer gently for 20 minutes. Thicken sauce with cornstarch which has been mixed into a paste with a little water. Simmer until sauce thickens. Serve over rice. **Serves: 6**

Rutgers University

# Shrimp Pilau

1 onion
4 cloves
1 cinnamon stick (broken into pieces)
4 cardamom seeds (split apart, discard shells)
1½ cups rice
3 cups chicken broth
½ teaspoon salt
1 teaspoon turmeric
1 can shrimp, drained
¼ cup raisins
¼ cup cashews

Sauté onions, cloves, cinnamon, and cardamom in butter until onion is translucent. Remove spices from butter with a slotted spoon and add rice. Sauté until rice is golden (about 5 minutes). Add salt and broth and simmer tightly covered until broth is absorbed and rice is tender (about 20 minutes). Add turmeric, shrimp, raisins, and cashews and toss to mix with rice. Cover and cook on low heat until shrimp is hot. Serve with sour cream. **Serves: 2-3**

UNIVERSITY OF DELAWARE
# Fish Scallop

*Use any fish fillets.*

2 pounds fish fillets
1 onion, chopped
1 ½ tablespoons flour
2 cups sour cream
½ cup Swiss cheese, grated
2 tablespoons butter
2 tablespoons sherry (optional)
2 tablespoons *each* currants and walnuts
½ teaspoon cinnamon
½ teaspoon allspice
1 teaspoon salt
½ teaspoon pepper
1 cup buttered bread crumbs (bread crumbs
    mixed with melted butter)

Preheat oven to 375° F. Dust fish with flour and brown lightly in butter on both sides. Place in buttered casserole in layers with sauce spooned onto each layer.

**Sauce**: Sauté onions until translucent. Mix flour with sour cream and add along with all other ingredients, except bread crumbs, to onions. Mix well. When fish and sauce are all in casserole, cover with bread crumbs and bake 45 minutes. **Serves: 4**

UNIVERSITY OF NORTHERN COLORADO
# Tuna-Vegetable Mix

*This is quick, but good. Any number can eat.*

brown rice
peas
corn
tunafish (canned)
onion salt
salt and pepper to taste

Cook rice, peas, and corn separately. Heat tunafish in a little butter with onion salt. Mix all together, salt and pepper to taste. Serve on plates; dump tunafish on top. **Serves: Depends on quantity**

BOSTON COLLEGE

# Baked Stuffed Haddock

1½ pounds fillet of haddock slices
shrimp (one for each haddock slice)
2 tablespoons toasted sesame seeds
1 cup butter, melted
½ teaspoon turmeric
½ cup white wine (optional)
dash salt, pepper
bread crumbs

Preheat oven to 350° F. On each slice of fish place 1 shrimp, a tiny pat of butter, and some sesame seeds. Roll up and skewer with toothpick. Lay rolled-up fish in buttered casserole. Combine melted butter, turmeric, wine, salt, and pepper. If there are any sesame seeds left, add them, too. Sprinkle over fish. Cover with bread crumbs that have been mixed with melted butter. Surface should be *completely* covered with bread crumbs.

Bake uncovered in oven about 30 minutes or until crumbs are quite brown. Allow 2 slices to a person. **Serves: 2-3**

UNIVERSITY OF NORTH CAROLINA, CHAPEL HILL

# Patty's Jambalaya

1 large onion, finely chopped
2 tablespoons shortening
2 tablespoons flour
1 pound hot sausage, cut in 1" slices
1 8-ounce can tomato sauce
1½ pounds shrimp, preferably fresh
    (or 16-ounce can)
1 garlic clove, minced
½ bell pepper, chopped
3 tablespoons parsley
2 cups water
salt and pepper to taste

Sauté onion in shortening in heavy pot until translucent. Add flour and stir over medium-low heat until light brown. Add sausage and shrimp and brown. Add tomato sauce, water, bell pepper, garlic, parsley, salt, and pepper. Cover and simmer for approximately 30 minutes. Spoon over hot cooked rice. **Serves: 8-10**

UNIVERSITY OF MARYLAND

# Baked Herbed Fish

1 package frozen spinach
3 tablespoons almonds, minced
1 pound fish fillets (any type)
½ cup butter, melted
1 teaspoon or more tarragon
salt and pepper to taste

Preheat oven to 375° F. Cook spinach as directed on package, with only half the amount of water and a pat of butter. Drain but reserve cooking liquid. Mix spinach with almonds and put on bottom of baking dish. Lay fish on top of spinach, and pour on melted butter which has been mixed with spinach liquid and tarragon. Salt and pepper to taste. Cover and bake 30-45 minutes.

Best served with little roast potatoes which can be roasted at the same time or with very dry white rice. **Serves: 3-4**

CURTIS INSTITUTE OF MUSIC

# Tunafish Casserole

1 package spaghetti
1 can tunafish, drained
2 cups peas (canned are all right)
½ cup onions, chopped
½ cup green peppers, chopped
2 tablespoons lemon juice
2 cups white sauce (made with light cream)
½ pound mushrooms
½ teaspoon curry powder
1 teaspoon sherry (optional)

Preheat oven to 375° F. Boil spaghetti. When cooked, drain and put in casserole with crumbled tunafish. Add rest of the ingredients and mix all up. Cover and bake about 45 minutes. **Serves: 4**

# Baked Flounder in Sour Cream

*A fish dish for when you tire of breading and frying it.*

fillets of fish (flounder, etc.)
butter
salt, pepper, paprika
mayonnaise
sour cream
mushrooms, sliced

Preheat oven to 350° F. Grease shallow baking dish. Dot fish with butter after laying in dish. Sprinkle with seasoning. Mix mayonnaise and sour cream in 1:2 proportions. Make enough of this to cover the fish—we like to smother it! Bake for at least 1 hour, adding the mushrooms on top during the last 15 minutes. **Serves: Depends on quantity**

# Salmon and Mushroom Casserole

1 can salmon, drained
4 cups brown rice, cooked
2 cups white sauce
1 pound mushrooms, sliced
3 cups broccoli, chopped
½ cup cheddar cheese, diced
½ cup raisins, moist or soaked 5 minutes in
    hot water

Preheat oven to 375° F. Throw it all in a greased casserole dish. Mix thoroughly with fork. Cover and bake for about 45 minutes. **Serves: 4-6**

# Fish Fillets in White Wine

Preheat oven to 350° F. Rub any fillet or fish steak with fresh lemon. Place in shallow glass baking dish. Sprinkle on salt, pepper, paprika, parsley, and lemon juice. Add white wine (up to ⅓ cup, depending on amount of fish). Dot fish with butter. Bake 10-15 minutes, until fish is flaky. Serve with enough sauce to moisten.

# Notes & Recipes

# VEGETABLES

**Recipes included and the main ingredients needed.**

THERESE'S SISTER'S GOURMET GREEN BEANS
Green beans, mushrooms, almonds

TANGY GREEN BEANS
Green beans, bacon, onion

GREEN BEANS IN TOMATO SAUCE
Green beans, onion, tomato paste

GREEN BEANS WITH SOUR CREAM
Green beans, Swiss cheese, almonds, onion, sour cream

SAUTÉED GREEN BEANS
Green beans, sesame seeds

FRIED CHINESE CABBAGE
Chinese cabbage

VIENNESE CABBAGE CASSEROLE
Cabbage, onion, sour cream, bacon fat

EGGPLANT PARMIGIANA
Eggplant, mozzarella, tomato sauce

SCALLOPED VEGETABLES
Potatoes, onions, assorted vegetables

SPINACH AND MUSHROOM CASSEROLE
Spinach, mushrooms, onion, white sauce

BROILED EGGPLANT
Eggplant, tomato sauce

FRIED CUCUMBERS
Cucumbers, eggs, cornmeal

SUE'S STUFFED MUSHROOMS
Mushrooms, celery, onions

RATATOUILLE
Eggplant, zucchini, tomatoes, onion

SPINACH PUDDING
Spinach, milk, eggs

POTATO PANCAKE
Potatoes, eggs, onions

VELVET YAMS
Yams

QUICK-FRY VEGETABLES
Fresh mixed vegetables

ZUCCHINI-TOMATO QUICKIE
Zucchini, tomatoes, onion

BAKED CARROTS AND YAMS
Yams, carrots, eggs, milk

ORANGE-YAM CASSEROLE
Yams, oranges, orange juice, sherry

LEFTOVER (OR NOT) BAKED YAMS
Yams

QUICK AND EASY CASSEROLE
Zucchini or eggplant, tomatoes, green peppers, onions, sharp cheese, cashews or almonds

SPINACH WITH SOUR CREAM
Spinach, sour cream

# VEGETABLES

### SPINACH AND CHEESE SQUARES
Eggs, whole wheat flour, cottage cheese, cheddar cheese, spinach, wheat germ

### QUICK SPINACH
Onion, mustard seed, spinach, mushrooms, oil

### SHREDDED ZUCCHINI
Zucchini

### QUICK VEGGIE-RATT
Onions, green peppers, carrot, eggplant, canned tomatoes

### ZINGY CARROTS
Carrots, lemon juice, oregano, garlic, black olives

### SANDRA'S FAMOUS CORN PUDDING
Cream-style corn, flour, eggs

### FALL VEGETABLE BAKE
Potatoes, butternut squash, zucchini, celery, onion, broccoli, snow peas or fresh peas, green beans, Parmesan cheese

### STUFFED ZUCCHINI
Zucchini, olive oil, garlic, pine nuts, rice, wheat germ, tomatoes, herbs, Parmesan cheese

Vegetables are cheap, tasty, and provide a welcome variety to the menu. Some are very versatile—almost all can be eaten both raw and cooked. The simplest way of preparing a vegetable—boiled in as little water as possible and served with butter and salt—can't be beat. But there are many other good ways and students sent me more vegetable recipes than any other kind. Since many of them are vegetarians, they have gone to a lot of trouble to make their meals interesting. If you have a favorite that is not included, I'd very much like to hear about it. Students seem to be vegetarians for one of two reasons—some through conviction, some because meat is too expensive for their budget. The lower cost of a vegetarian diet is a big advantage. If you are careful, you can eat almost as well as a meat eater for a lot less. I, for one, would miss meat very much.

Vegetarians have one big disadvantage—the problem of getting sufficient complete protein in their diet. Eggs added to vegetable and pasta dishes are a satisfactory meat substitute; soybeans, all dried beans, cheese, nuts, and milk all add valuable protein of various kinds, but you have to know what you are doing or you will gradually lose energy and health. A food may contain protein but not the right kind. So you have to be really up on nutrition—on the different kinds of protein, how much of each the body requires, etc. If you are a vegetarian, plan your food intake carefully. If you just assume that all vegetables are good for you and it doesn't matter what combination of them you eat, you will find yourself in trouble. The effects of an unbalanced diet can be slow; you may not realize what is happening right away.

Most of these vegetable dishes are quick and easy. However, be sure to add preparation time (for peeling, chopping, etc.) to cooking time when you are making your meal plans.

UNIVERSITY OF COLORADO

# Therese's Sister's Gourmet Green Beans

1 pound fresh or frozen green beans
½ cup mushrooms, sliced
2 tablespoons almonds, slivered
2 tablespoons oil
½ teaspoon thyme
¼ teaspoon sage
grated cheese

Sauté beans, mushrooms, and almonds in hot oil. Add seasoning and toss. Cook until beans are crisp-tender. Douse with grated cheese, gush it all together. Serve hot. **Serves: 4**

UNIVERSITY OF COLORADO

# Tangy Green Beans

1 pound green beans, cut up
2 slices bacon, diced
½ onion, minced
¼ cup vinegar
salt and pepper to taste

Cook beans in boiling, salted water for 20 minutes. Meanwhile, fry bacon until crisp. Take out bacon and saute onion in bacon fat until golden. Add bacon and vinegar. Heat to boiling. When beans are done, pour bacon and sauce over beans, season, and toss. **Serves: 4-5**

VASSAR COLLEGE

# Green Beans in Tomato Sauce

butter or oil
1 onion, diced
2 cups water
1 beef bouillon cube
½ teaspoon salt
¼ teaspoon pepper
¼ teaspoon cinnamon
½ teaspoon garlic salt
1 pound green beans, cut in 1" pieces
4 ounces tomato paste

Heat butter or oil in saucepan and brown onions. Add water and bring to a boil. Add bouillon cube and seasoning. Stir. Add beans and tomato paste. Stir until thoroughly mixed. Simmer 30 minutes. **Serves: 6**

UNIVERSITY OF DENVER

# Green Beans with Sour Cream

*We love this way of cooking beans. I suggest you prepare the vegetables and put them in the casserole before you make the sauce. Any kind of cheese and any nuts you like are okay.*

1 onion, minced
2 pounds French-style green beans, cooked
1 teaspoon sugar
2 tablespoons butter
1 tablespoon flour
1 teaspoon salt
½ teaspoon pepper
½ pint sour cream
2 tablespoons Swiss cheese, grated
2 tablespoons almonds, chopped

Preheat oven to 400° F. Mix onions, beans, and sugar and put in buttered casserole. Melt butter in pan until foamy. Take off burner and stir in flour, adding gradually. Put back on burner for one minute, stirring occasionally. Add salt, pepper, and sour cream. Heat but do not boil. Spoon sauce over vegetables and toss lightly until it is all mixed up. Sprinkle with grated cheese and almonds. Bake for 15-20 minutes. **Serves: 4**

GODDARD COLLEGE

# Sautéed Green Beans

2 tablespoons olive oil or butter
1 pound green beans, cut in 1″ pieces
1 garlic clove, minced
1 teaspoon sesame seeds
¼ teaspoon nutmeg

Heat butter or oil in skillet until it sizzles when bean is dropped into it. Add all ingredients and toss lightly to coat them with butter or oil. Cook, tossing lightly from time to time until desired consistency (5-10 minutes). You can cook them to crisp, stir-fried consistency like Chinese vegetables, or until tender, like American vegetables. Taste as you go along and see at what point they suit you. **Serves: 5-6**

UNIVERSITY OF DENVER

# Fried Chinese Cabbage

1 Chinese cabbage
1 garlic clove, minced
2 tablespoons olive oil
salt and pepper to taste

Wash cabbage and shake thoroughly dry. It's even better to wash it in the morning and stand it upside down to drain. Then cook it in the afternoon when you are hungry. Cut off bottom of cabbage and chop the rest up coarsely. Sauté garlic lightly in hot oil. Add cabbage and toss for 8-10 minutes. Season. **Serves: 3-4**

UNIVERSITY OF MAINE
# Viennese Cabbage Casserole

9 cups cabbage, shredded
¼ cup bacon fat or oil
2 tablespoons onion, finely chopped
1 cup sour cream
2 teaspoons salt
2 teaspoons paprika

Preheat oven to 350° F. Sauté cabbage in hot bacon fat or oil 5 minutes. Add onion and seasoning. Put in 1-quart casserole and spoon sour cream over the top. Bake for 30 minutes. **Serves: 6**

COLUMBIA UNIVERSITY
# Eggplant Parmigiana

1 medium eggplant, cut in 1″ slices
2 cups bread crumbs
3 tablespoons olive oil
2 garlic cloves, minced
1 small can tomato sauce
1 cup mozzarella cheese, diced
3 tablespoons grated Parmesan cheese

Preheat oven to 325° F. Bread eggplant and fry in hot olive oil with garlic. Place in flat pan. Pour tomato sauce over eggplant and dot with mozzarella. Bake for 30 minutes. Five minutes before it is done, sprinkle with Parmesan cheese and put under broiler until cheese is melted. **Serves: 3-4**

BOSTON UNIVERSITY
# Scalloped Vegetables

*You can use just potatoes and onions, if that's all there is. The amount of ingredients is approximate as long as you use enough potatoes.*

3 cups potatoes, sliced
whole wheat flour
6 carrots, sliced
6 small onions, sliced
3 stalks celery, chopped
3 green onions, chopped
1½-3 cups milk
1 teaspoon salt
1 teaspoon paprika

Preheat oven to 350° F. Dredge potatoes in flour. Arrange vegetables in layers with potatoes forming every other layer. A low casserole or round baking dish is good. Dot layers with butter as you go along. Heat milk with seasonings and pour over vegetables. Bake covered 30 minutes; if you don't have a cover, use foil. Then bake uncovered for another 30-45 minutes until vegetables are tender and milk is fairly thickened and absorbed. **Serves: 6**

VASSAR COLLEGE

# Spinach and Mushroom Casserole

2 pounds spinach, fresh or 2 packages, frozen
3 tablespoons onion, grated
1 pound mushrooms, (caps and stems) sliced
4 tablespoons Swiss cheese, grated
2½ cups white sauce

Preheat oven to 325° F. If spinach is fresh, wash thoroughly to remove sand. Allow plenty of time for this. Drain well and chop coarsely. Or thaw frozen spinach and drain well. Arrange spinach, onions, and mushrooms in alternate layers, starting with spinach. Add sauce for each three layers, ending with a topping of sauce. Sprinkle with cheese and bake for 45 minutes. **Serves: 4**

COLUMBIA UNIVERSITY

# Broiled Eggplant

1 medium eggplant, cut in ½″ thick slices
1 can tomato sauce
1 teaspoon basil
1 teaspoon oregano
salt and pepper to taste

Preheat broiler. Involves simply shoving in broiler, cooking 5 minutes, turning, pouring on sauce (mixed with spices and seasoning), and broiling another 5-10 minutes. Leave skin on the eggplant. It's healthy. **Serves: 3-4**

UNIVERSITY OF NEW MEXICO

# Fried Cucumbers

*If you're looking for a different tasting vegetable, try this one.*

6 cucumbers, sliced
2 eggs, beaten
1½ cups cornmeal
4 tablespoons butter
salt and pepper to taste
sour cream or yogurt

Put cucumbers on paper toweling as you slice them. Pat tops dry, then dip both sides in beaten egg, then in cornmeal. Fry quickly in hot butter until brown, turning once. Drain on paper towels if necessary, and serve with sour cream or yogurt on the side. **Serves: 4-6**

UNIVERSITY OF NEW HAMPSHIRE

## Sue's Stuffed Mushrooms

*It looks complicated when you write it all out
but it's very quick to do!*

1 pound whole, fresh mushrooms
2½ tablespoons butter
1 slice stale bread or 1 cup plain croutons
½ stalk celery, chopped
¼ cup onions, chopped
salt and pepper to taste

Preheat oven to 350° F. Wipe mushroom caps
with damp paper towel. Twist off stems. Scoop
out gills (underside of mushroom cap) with a
small spoon. Heat ½ tablespoon butter in skillet.
Lay scooped-out mushroom caps upside down in
skillet; brown until juice rises in each cap. Remove and keep hot. Chop up mushroom stems.
Mix bread, celery, onions, mushroom stems, and
scooped-out gills. Add salt and pepper. Add remaining butter to skillet and heat. Put bread
mixture in skillet, stir and heat thoroughly. Fill
mushroom caps with heated bread mixture and
bake 10 minutes. The tiny mushrooms don't stuff
well. Can also be used as an hors d'oeuvre.
**Serves: 2**

PRESCOTT COLLEGE

## Ratatouille

1 medium eggplant
3 small zucchini
3 firm tomatoes
1 large onion
4-6 tablespoons olive oil
3 cloves garlic, minced
½ teaspoon oregano
vegetable salt to taste
grated Parmesan cheese

Preheat oven to 300° F. Peel and cut both eggplant and zucchini into 1½" cubes. Chop tomatoes
coarsely. Slice onion. Pour oil into large skillet;
when hot, sauté zucchini and eggplant until lightly
brown. Remove from pan. Lower heat and add
onions, tomatoes, garlic, and seasoning. Simmer
until onions are limp. Place all ingredients in
casserole, sprinkle with cheese, cover and bake
for 1 hour. Serve hot the first time, cold the next.
**Serves: 4-6**

VASSAR COLLEGE

# Spinach Pudding

2 10-ounce packages frozen chopped spinach
2 tablespoons butter
¼ cup all-purpose flour
¾ cup milk
2 teaspoons salt
½ teaspoon pepper
¼-½ teaspoon nutmeg
3 eggs, beaten

Preheat oven to 350° F. Cook spinach as directed on package but without adding water. Drain thoroughly. Melt butter in a heavy pan; add flour, stirring constantly. Stir in milk gradually; add seasonings and spinach. Stir in beaten egg. Spinach should be well mixed and well coated with everything. Turn into greased 1½ quart casserole. Place in pan of hot water and bake for 30 minutes. Serve right from casserole or unmold and serve on warm plate with hot heavy cream (optional). **Serves: 6**

CURTIS INSTITUTE OF MUSIC

# Potato Pancake

3 potatoes, grated
¾ cup onions, chopped
2 eggs
1 teaspoon oil
salt and pepper to taste

Mix potatoes and onions together and add 2 beaten eggs. Blend well. Pour into *small* skillet, well-greased and hot. To brown, quick-fry at high heat on both sides. Then put under broiler for 10 minutes. Season to taste. **Serves: 2**

PRESCOTT COLLEGE

# Velvet Yams

*Really, really good. Really, really simple.*

Yams, the fat red velvet ones, are best baked in foil. Spread with butter first, then bake at 375° F oven, woodstove, fireplace, or campfire. Serve with salt and whipped sweet butter.

MILLS COLLEGE
## Quick-Fry Vegetables

**butter**
**chopped fresh mixed vegetables**

If you have a wok, this is the perfect pan. Otherwise use a heavy frying pan. Heat about 2 tablespoons of butter. Add bean sprouts, onions, green peppers, mushrooms, string beans, asparagus, broccoli, cauliflower, escarole, water chestnuts, hearts of palm or any other combination that appeals to you. For the last 30-60 seconds, add fresh spinach thoroughly washed and drained. All vegetables should be chopped or thinly sliced so they will cook fast. Cook only a few minutes until hot all the way through. Taste to be sure. Serve as is with seasoning or make sauce as follows:

**Sauce:** Just before serving, add 3 tablespoons soy sauce and a little cornstarch mixed to a paste in cold water. Cook a minute more until sauce gets thick and transparent. If it gets too thick, add a little water or chicken broth; too thin, add more cornstarch. Don't worry if it doesn't come out exactly right the first try. Serve over hot rice or noodles. **Serves: Depends on quantity**

UNIVERSITY OF DENVER
## Zucchini-Tomato Quickie

**butter**
**1 large onion, sliced**
**2 tomatoes, chopped**
**4-5 medium zucchini, sliced but not peeled**
**1 teaspoon oregano**
**salt to taste**

Heat butter in a large saucepan. Put in onion and cook until limp. Add tomato and zucchini. Season. Cover pan and cook, stirring occasionally until zucchini is tender but not soggy. No water needed—the zucchini has enough water in it.

You can make this a main dish by browning a pound of hamburger with the onions and then making everything else according to the rest of the recipe. **Serves: 4**

UNIVERSITY OF CALIFORNIA AT LOS ANGELES

# Baked Carrots and Yams

1½ pounds carrots
1 pound yams
4 medium eggs
1 cup milk
3 tablespoons melted butter
½ stick safflower margarine

Peel and parboil carrots. Cook yams in their jackets, then peel them. Grate carrots and yams. Beat eggs and milk in a mixing bowl, then add:

4 tablespoons brown sugar
1 teaspoon sea salt
¼ teaspoon ground cinnamon

Preheat oven to 300° F. Add shredded carrots and yams and mix well. Pour into baking dish lined with butter. Dot with margarine and bake for 30 minutes. **Serves: 6**

WILLIAMS COLLEGE

# Orange-Yam Casserole

*This makes a special company dish—good with baked ham or chicken.*

8 yams
¾ cup melted butter
½ cup sherry (optional)
1 cup orange juice
1 tablespoon orange rind, grated
salt and pepper to taste
½ cup honey
3 oranges peeled and divided into segments
¼ cup brown sugar, packed

Preheat oven to 350° F. Put whole, unpeeled yams into large pan of boiling water. Boil until fork pierces easily into center—about 30 minutes depending on size of yams. Peel and mash yams in large bowl with *almost all* of the butter, sherry, orange juice, and orange rind. Add seasoning and drizzle in honey, stirring to get it all through. Put in buttered casserole and arrange orange segments decoratively on top. Dissolve brown sugar in rest of orange juice, add sherry and rind and sprinkle over oranges. Bake for 30 minutes and serve hot. Heats up easily for another night. **Serves: 6-8**

PRESCOTT COLLEGE

# Leftover (or Not) Baked Yams

*If you have some baked yams left over, or even if not, make this with cooked yams.*

Slice the yams, fry them as patties in hot butter. Then, when brown on both sides serve with honey, molasses, brown sugar, maple syrup, or whatever—and a dash of nutmeg, cinnamon, or mace. Ginger is good, too.

UNIVERSITY OF CALIFORNIA AT LOS ANGELES

# Quick and Easy Casserole

4 small zucchini or one small eggplant
4 tomatoes
2 green peppers
2 onions
1 pound sharp cheese, grated
cashews or almonds, chopped
small pieces of bread (optional)

Preheat oven to 375° F. In any large casserole, slice and aesthetically arrange the ingredients. Bake for 45 minutes. Serve with rice. **Serves: 4**

UNIVERSITY OF LOUISVILLE

# Spinach with Sour Cream

1½ cups sour cream
1 tablespoon onion salt
1 garlic clove, minced
2 packages frozen chopped spinach, cooked
    and drained until very dry
4 tablespoons sherry (optional)
½ teaspoon ginger
salt and pepper to taste
1 cup bread crumbs

Preheat oven to 350° F. Put sour cream, onion salt, and garlic in blender and blend. Or mix very, very thoroughly with fork. Add to all the other ingredients and mix thoroughly. Put in casserole, top with bread crumbs. Bake 25 minutes. **Serves: 4**

WESLEYAN UNIVERSITY

# Spinach and Cheese Squares

2 eggs
6 tablespoons whole wheat flour
2 cups cottage cheese
2 cups cheddar cheese, grated
1 pound fresh spinach, torn in pieces
2 tablespoons wheat germ
1 tablespoon melted butter
½ teaspoon salt

Preheat oven to 350° F. Beat eggs lightly. Add flour and mix well. Add cottage and cheddar cheeses, spinach, and salt. Mix together—hands work best for this—until completely mixed. Spoon into well-greased 8″ × 12″ baking dish. Combine melted butter and wheat germ and sprinkle over the top. Bake uncovered for about 45 minutes. **Serves: 4**

RUTGERS UNIVERSITY

# Quick Spinach

1 onion, chopped
1 tablespoon mustard seed
1 package fresh spinach, washed and coarsely chopped
1 cup mushrooms, sliced (stems, too)
⅓ cup corn, peanut, or olive oil

Sauté onion and mustard seed until onions are golden. Add spinach and mushrooms and cover. Cook until spinach is tender (not long). Serve with plain yogurt. **Serves: 2-3**

WILLIAM SMITH COLLEGE

# Shredded Zucchini

*Very, very quick and good!*

3-4 small zucchini
2 tablespoons butter or olive oil
salt and pepper to taste

Grate zucchini on coarse side of grater. Cook in hot butter or oil for about 3 minutes, tossing the whole time. Season with salt and freshly ground pepper. You can do the same thing with shredded carrots. Add ½ teaspoon of ginger or 1 teaspoon poppy or caraway seeds. **Serves: 3**

COLUMBIA UNIVERSITY

# Quick Veggie-Ratt

olive oil
1 cup onions, diced
1 cup green peppers, diced
1 medium carrot, minced
1-2 cups eggplant, diced
1 medium can whole tomatoes
minced garlic
salt and pepper to taste
oregano

Sauté onions, peppers, and carrots in oil in medium fry pan until wilted and almost brown. In a saucepan, combine tomatoes and seasonings to make sauce. Simmer sauce 10-15 minutes until thick. Add diced eggplant to vegetables and cook until soft. Add sauce to vegetables. Cover and simmer 10-20 minutes. Great with Italian bread. **Serves: 2-3**

INDIANA UNIVERSITY

# Zingy Carrots

*Everyone likes carrots this way.*

8 carrots, scraped and sliced
2 tablespoons olive oil
2 tablespoons lemon juice
1 teaspoon grated lemon rind
¼ teaspoon oregano
1 garlic clove, minced
½ cup black olives, chopped
salt to taste

Cook carrots until crisp-tender, about 10 minutes. Combine other ingredients in small saucepan and heat to boiling. When carrots are done, drain and pour sauce over them. This recipe works hot or cold. **Serves: 2-4**

UPSALA COLLEGE, WIRTHS CAMPUS

# Sandra's Famous Corn Pudding

*This recipe originated in West Virginia. I have scattered it through Kentucky and now New Jersey. It is foolproof, easy, and a real winner.*

2 cans cream-style corn
1 tablespoon sugar
1 teaspoon salt
2 tablespoons flour
¾ cup evaporated milk
3 tablespoons butter
4 eggs, beaten

Preheat oven to 350° F. Combine sugar, flour, and salt. Gradually add milk, stirring to blend. Add corn and eggs and mix. Pour into greased 1 ½-quart casserole. Dot with butter. Bake 1 hour or until eggs are set. **Serves: 4**

UNIVERSITY OF NEW HAMPSHIRE

# Fall Vegetable Bake

*Use only fresh vegetables.*

2 large or 3 small potatoes, cut in 1″ cubes (leave the skin on for extra flavor and nutrition)
½ large butternut squash, seeded, peeled, and cut in cubes
2 medium zucchini or yellow crookneck, cut in cubes
3 large stalks of celery, coarsely chopped
1 medium to large onion, diced
1 medium head of broccoli, cut in 1″ pieces
1 cup snow peas or fresh peas (optional)
1 cup green beans, chopped (optional)
¼ cup butter, approximately
2 tablespoons parsley
1 teaspoon basil
grated cheddar or Parmesan cheese

Preheat oven to 350° F. Combine all vegetables in a large dutch oven or deep casserole. Dot with butter and sprinkle with herbs. Cover and bake for 45-55 minutes or until potatoes are tender. Toss occasionally during cooking to distribute butter and herbs. Serve, sprinkling each portion with cheese. **Serves: 6**

BENNINGTON COLLEGE

# Stuffed Zucchini

6 medium zucchini
¼ cup olive oil
4 medium onions, chopped
3 garlic cloves, minced
¼ cup pine nuts
½ cup rice, cooked
3 tablespoons wheat germ
3 tomatoes, peeled and seeded, chopped
½ teaspoon fresh basil, minced
½ teaspoon fresh oregano, minced
½ cup fresh bread crumbs
½ cup grated Parmesan cheese
salt and pepper to taste

Preheat oven to 350° F. Cut ends off zucchini and slice in half lengthwise. Scoop out insides, leaving walls thick enough to hold stuffing. Set halves aside. Heat all but one tablespoon olive oil in skillet and sauté onions and garlic until onions are translucent. Add zucchini scooped from shells, tomatoes, pine nuts, and rice. Cover and cook until soft. Place zucchini halves in a baking dish filled ¾ inch deep with boiling water (or add water after the dish is in the oven). Spoon skillet mixture into zucchini shells. Mix herbs, seasoning, cheese, bread crumbs, and wheat germ with remaining olive oil. Spoon over filling, heaping high. Use your hands to mound it. If it doesn't stick together, add a little more oil. Bake for 30 minutes or until shell feels tender when you stick a fork in it (carefully). **Serves: 6**

**Variations**: You can use peanuts instead of pine nuts and can add hamburger (sautéed until all the pink is gone). Or lay thin strips of mozzarella over the filling before you put the topping on. This is a great dish for using up leftovers and the amounts don't matter. If you want to use larger zucchini, bake the shells for about 30 minutes in a slow oven (300° F) or they will never get tender; then fill them and proceed as above.

# RICE AND PASTA

### Recipes included and the chief ingredients needed.

BASIC BROWN RICE AND VEGETABLES
Brown rice, soy sauce, mixed fresh vegetables

YELLOW RICE
Rice, chicken broth, butter, saffron, curry, or turmeric

BROWN RICE PATTIES
Brown rice, carrots, onion, eggs, whole wheat flour

FRIED RICE
Rice, eggs, scallions or onions, bean sprouts, ham, soy sauce

CLAM SPAGHETTI
Spaghetti, clams, butter, wine, lemon juice, Parmesan cheese

SPAGHETTI WITH HOMEMADE MEAT SAUCE
Spaghetti, tomato sauce, tomato paste, ground beef, onion, garlic, parsley

SPINACH AND SPAGHETTI BAKE
Spinach, egg, sour cream, milk, Parmesan cheese, onion, Monterey Jack cheese, cooked spaghetti

SPAGHETTI ALLA CARBONARA
Spaghetti, eggs, Romano cheese, Parmesan cheese, bacon

SAVORY RICE
Brown or white rice and one of the following: mushrooms, pine nuts, pineapple, pimientos, peas, ham, chicken, parsley, onion

MIKE'S MEATLESS SPAGHETTI ALLA CARBONARA
Onions, garlic, mushrooms, red peppers, wrinkled black olives, walnuts, herbs

KIM'S LASAGNA
Ground beef, mozzarella cheese, lasagna noodles, garlic, tomato paste, onion, parsley, cottage cheese, Parmesan cheese, eggs

SUPER QUICK MACARONI AND CHEESE
Macaroni, American or similar cheese, milk

# RICE AND PASTA

Rice and pasta dishes are very useful, inexpensive, and substitute interestingly for potatoes. They are especially indispensable for those days when the budget is low because the amount of meat, vegetables, or cheese used is flexible; you can add more or less depending on what you can afford. Because of this flexibility, most of these recipes are foolproof. Almost any proportion of main ingredients tastes good as long as you have enough sauce. If you misjudged and need more sauce in a hurry, add more olive oil or butter, whichever the recipe calls for, and toss thoroughly. In substituting brown rice for white rice, see the table of substitutions. In general, you will need to use more water and allow a longer cooking time.

UNIVERSITY OF CALIFORNIA AT LOS ANGELES

# Basic Brown Rice and Vegetables

4 cups brown rice, uncooked
6 cups water
2 tablespoons soy sauce

Preheat oven to 350° F. Mix together and bake for 1½ hours, covered. This gives you your basic rice and it will come out with a fuller, nuttier flavor and dryer texture than boiled rice.

*To cook vegetables*: Sauté in 2 tablespoons of butter or oil any combination of chopped up vegetables such as scallions, bean sprouts, alfalfa sprouts, zucchini, green peppers, tomato, green beans, carrots, celery, etc. Do not sauté vegetables more than 5 minutes or they will lose their crispness. Add a bit of soy sauce to the pan at the last minute to enrich the sauce; serve over rice. Don't salt this until you taste it—the soy should be enough. May be garnished with grated jack cheese or even yogurt. Grated nuts, almonds, or cashews add protein and variety. **Serves: 6-8**

RICE UNIVERSITY

# Yellow Rice

*This is fabulous with broiled chicken. We make it three ways by varying the seasoning. Each seasoning has its own color and taste, so you'll have to try them all to see which one you like best.*

2 tablespoons butter
1 teaspoon salt
½ teaspoon pepper
¼ teaspoon saffron *or* 2 tablespoons curry *or* 2 tablespoons turmeric
1 cup rice, uncooked
2 cups hot chicken broth

Melt butter in pan and add seasoning. Stir to blend. Add rice and stir to coat with butter and seasoning. Cook five minutes, stirring occasionally so rice does not stick or burn. Add hot chicken broth; stir well once. Cover tightly and cook without looking on *low heat* for 25 minutes. Liquid should be completely absorbed and rice should be golden and tender. **Serves: 2**

University of California at Irvine

# Brown Rice Patties

8 cups brown rice, cooked
½ cup parsley, minced
1 cup carrots, grated
½ cup onion, minced
1 clove garlic, minced
1 teaspoon salt
2 eggs, beaten
½ cup whole wheat flour
1 cup oil (sesame is especially tasty)

Combine all ingredients except oil, mixing well. Form into patties, pressing firmly with hands and making uniform in size so they will all be ready at the same time. You won't be able to get all of them in one skillet, so keep the first ones hot by covering them with foil or placing them in a warm oven (if you have one). Heat oil in skillet and fry patties until brown on both sides (you should turn them only once). **Makes: 12 patties**

   **Note**: If you don't have brown rice, only white, add chopped peanuts (about ½ cup) to make more flavorful.

University of Denver

# Fried Rice

*No matter how broke you are, vary your meals. If you're serving an ordinary meal to a friend, put candles on the table. It makes it more special.*

4 cups rice, cooked
⅓ cup oil (peanut oil is traditional)
2 eggs
3 tablespoons soy sauce
½ cup scallions or onion, minced
½ cup bean sprouts
½ cup ham, chopped

Leftover rice is fine. Sauté cooked rice in oil until lightly browned. Keep stirring—don't let it stick on the bottom of the pan if you can help it. Add eggs and soy sauce and cook, stirring until eggs are solid and all broken up in the rice. Add other ingredients and cook until everything is hot—not very long. **Serves: 4**

## ᴧ Spaghetti

*Whole meal takes 15 minutes to make and it's a company dish!*

1 package spaghetti
1 stick butter
1 can minced clams
2 tablespoons parsley, dried or fresh, minced
2 tablespoons onion salt
1 teaspoon garlic powder
grated Parmesan cheese
½ teaspoon black pepper
½ teaspoon salt
¼ cup white wine or vermouth (optional)
2 teaspoons lemon juice

Put spaghetti in boiling salted water and cook until done. Melt butter in small saucepan and add the clam juice drained from the can of clams. Add parsley, onion salt, garlic, pepper, and salt. Cook on very low heat. Five minutes before spaghetti is ready, add wine, lemon juice, and clams. Drain spaghetti. Put cheese on bottom of individual bowls and place spaghetti over it. Then spoon sauce over each serving. **Serves: 4**

VASSAR COLLEGE

# Spaghetti with Homemade Meat Sauce

*Make sauce first. It takes longer and it doesn't matter if it simmers lots more than an hour. This is a very meaty sauce—practically a meal in itself. You could use half as much meat if you need to.*

1 medium onion, diced
2 tablespoons olive oil
1 pound ground hamburger
12 ounce can tomato paste
24 ounce can tomato sauce
2 cloves garlic, pressed
3 tablespoons parsley, minced
1 teaspoon oregano
1 teaspoon salt
½ teaspoon pepper
1 teaspoon basil
1 package spaghetti

Brown meat and drain fat. Set aside. Sauté onion in olive oil. When onions turn translucent, add browned meat to olive oil-onion mixture. Add rest of ingredients (except spaghetti) and simmer for 1 hour, at least. Cook and drain spaghetti and serve with sauce and grated cheese. **Serves: 6**

UNIVERSITY OF CALIFORNIA AT DAVIS
# Spinach and Spaghetti Bake

*This casserole doesn't look very appealing, as many of my friends attest to as I'm making or serving it, but almost everyone loves it—even those who hate spinach.*

10 ounce package frozen spinach, cooked and
    drained
1 egg, beaten
½ cup sour cream
¼ cup milk
2 tablespoons grated Parmesan cheese
2 tablespoons onion, minced
½ teaspoon salt
dash pepper
2 cups Monterey Jack cheese, shredded
4 ounces (2 cups) cooked spaghetti
2 tablespoons grated Parmesan cheese

Preheat oven to 350° F. Combine egg, sour cream, and milk. Add 2 tablespoons Parmesan cheese, onion, salt, and pepper. Blend and add Jack cheese, then spinach, then spaghetti. Toss lightly and spoon into ungreased 10″ × 6″ × 2″ pan. Sprinkle with remaining 2 tablespoons Parmesan cheese. Cover tightly with foil and bake for 15 minutes. Uncover and bake another 15-20 minutes. **Serves: 4-5**

PRESCOTT COLLEGE
# Spaghetti alla Carbonara

*We would rather eat at home than in the college cafeteria because we like to eat food that has been prepared by people who care about what they are eating and what they are creating.*

spaghetti
bacon
olive oil
eggs
grated Romano cheese
grated Parmesan cheese
salt and pepper to taste

Cook spaghetti. While spaghetti is cooking, sauté bacon until crisp, then combine with a little olive oil. Drain off some bacon fat. Separate yolks and whites of eggs. Use one egg for each person you are planning to serve. Beat yolks and add a little of the whites—less than half of what you have. Grate lots of cheese into the eggs and add pepper till everything is black. When spaghetti is cooked and drained, add beaten eggs and bacon and toss. Top with more grated cheese when serving. **Serves: Depends on quantity**

UNIVERSITY OF TEXAS

# Savory Rice

*Use either brown or white rice, depending on your preference. Cook as you usually do (or follow directions on package). When done, add to the hot cooked rice any one of the following:*

sautéed sliced mushrooms
pine nuts
minced pineapple and mint flakes
minced pimientos and cooked peas, heated
    with bits of cooked ham, chicken or both
    and bit of tarragon
minced parsley and minced onions

Toss well and serve. This is so cheap you can even have it for lunch. **Serves: Depends on quantity**

MASSACHUSETTS INSTITUTE OF TECHNOLOGY

# Mike's Meatless Spaghetti alla Carbonara

3 medium onions, chopped
2 garlic cloves, minced
1 pound mushrooms, thinly sliced
3 red peppers, roasted, peeled and chopped
½ cup wrinkled black olives, pitted and
    chopped
⅓ cup chopped walnuts
¼ cup olive oil *or* butter
salt, pepper, thyme, oregano, and basil
eggs
grated Parmesan cheese

Sauté onions and garlic until onions are translucent. Add mushrooms, herbs, vegetables, nuts, and seasonings and sauté until mushrooms are tender. Do not let mushrooms brown; sauce should be light in color. Set mushroom sauce aside or refrigerate. You can make a lot of sauce and refrigerate it for a week, to be used off and on, but bring whatever amount you plan to use to room temperature. Cook whatever amount of spaghetti you want. Drain and put in warmed bowl. Add one egg per side dish serving to lukewarm mushroom mixture and toss. The sauce will be fairly thick. Spoon over hot spaghetti and toss. Serve immediately with Parmesan cheese. If serving as a main dish, add two eggs per serving. **Serves: 6**

TEXAS CHRISTIAN UNIVERSITY

# Kim's Lasagna

*This is one of my very favorite recipes. It makes one meal to which we are certain to have guests who "just happen to be in the neighborhood." All of our friends love it.* One caution—*let the lasagna stand at least 10 minutes before cutting or you may wind up snipping stringy cheese with the scissors (as we did!).*

1 pound ground beef
1 garlic clove, minced
1 tablespoon basil
1 ½ teaspoons salt
2 6-ounce cans tomato paste
½ cup onion, minced
snipped fresh parsley or parsley flakes
10 ounces lasagna noodles
1 pound mozzarella cheese, thinly sliced

CHEESE FILLING:
3 cups creamy cottage cheese
½ cup grated Parmesan
2 tablespoons fresh parsley or parsley flakes
2 beaten eggs
2 teaspoons salt
½ teaspoon pepper

Preheat oven to 375° F. Brown meat. Drain fat. Add all other ingredients, except mozzarella cheese and cheese filling, to meat. Simmer 30 minutes, stirring occasionally. Cook lasagna noodles until tender. Mix cheese filling ingredients well. In large baking dish, put a layer of ½ noodles, ½ cheese filling, ½ mozzarella, ½ meat sauce. Repeat each layer. Bake for 30 minutes. Let stand 10 minutes before cutting. **Serves: 12**

UNIVERSITY OF COLORADO

# Super Quick Macaroni and Cheese

*No baking—takes about 15 minutes.*

Cook macaroni and drain well. Cut up American or any soft cheese into ¼" cubes. Add to hot noodles, stir until just melted. Add hot milk until desired consistency and "juicy" enough. Add salt, pepper, and butter (very important) to taste. Serve!

# SALADS

**Recipes included and the chief ingredients needed.**

### BEAN SALAD
Red kidney beans, white kidney beans, green beans, lima beans

### HOT POTATO SALAD
Potatoes, bacon, onion, parsley

### COLESLAW
Cabbage, carrots, dill, celery seed, sweet pickles

### CHILLED POTATO SALAD
Potatoes, celery, green pepper, pimientos, scallions, eggs, sweet pickles

### CHEF'S SALAD
Ham, chicken, eggs (optional), cheese, salad greens or spinach

### GUACAMOLE
Avocados, onion, tomato, lemon juice

### ORANGE-ONION SALAD
Oranges, onions, lettuce

### HEARTY VEGETABLE SALAD
Lentils, beef broth, parsley, celery, zucchini, red pepper, onion, garlic

### HOT CHEF'S SALAD
Green pepper, cooked beef, cooked chicken, onion, eggplant, brussel sprouts, cabbage, tomato paste, cheese, wheat germ

### TABOULI
Parsley, bulgur, scallions, tomatoes, lemon or orange juice

### INSPIRATION SALAD
A combination of leftovers—whatever you have on hand that inspires you

### LYNN'S COLESLAW
Cabbage, carrot, green pepper, zucchini

### POTATO SALAD WITH YOGURT
Potatoes, yogurt, carrots, cucumbers

# SALADS

Americans are often thought of as subsisting primarily on a diet of "meat-and-potatoes." While it is true that we eat a higher proportion of meat per capita than other countries, vegetables and salads are beginning to represent a much larger part of our menu. The French have always considered a mixed green salad the height of high cuisine, but we usually like something more in a salad than just greens. When dips became popular, everyone discovered that almost all vegetables taste good raw; as we became more sophisticated about nutrition, we found that raw vegetables not only taste good, they are good for you.

Of course, every thrifty homemaker long ago discovered that last night's vegetables are good cold in today's salads, and mixed bean salads are so popular that they are now sold, already made, in cans. A good salad dressing is, however, very important. Fortunately, the really great dressings are simple to make. You can't beat olive oil and vinegar plus a little salt, pepper, and garlic. Sour cream forms the base of good dressings, as does yogurt, and if you want to take just a little more trouble, there is homemade mayonnaise—a far cry from the commercial product.

A salad can be a meal, a side dish, or a separate course, so adapt the quantities in the following recipes according to how you want to serve them.

RICE UNIVERSITY
# Bean Salad

1 cup *each* cooked: red kidney beans, white
    kidney beans, green
    beans, lima beans
1 onion, chopped
3 tablespoons olive oil
3 tablespoons vinegar
1 teaspoon sugar
½ teaspoon dry mustard
1 teaspoon salt
½ teaspoon fresh ground pepper

Make dressing and toss thoroughly. Refrigerate at least 1 hour before serving. **Serves: 4**

UNIVERSITY OF MINNESOTA
# Hot Potato Salad

6 potatoes
4 slices bacon
1 onion, diced
1 tablespoon parsley, minced
⅓ cup vinegar
1 tablespoon sugar
1 teaspoon salt
½ teaspoon pepper

Cook potatoes in skins. Peel and dice. Meanwhile, fry bacon until crisp. Mix parsley, vinegar, sugar, salt, and pepper, heat to boiling. Crumble bacon into hot potatoes. Add onions and vinegar mixture. Toss lightly until thoroughly mixed. Serve hot. **Serves: 3**

UNIVERSITY OF DENVER
# Coleslaw

*We have a saying, "coleslaw today—mushrooms tomorrow," because coleslaw is so easy on the budget. Easy on time, too.*

Grate half a head of cabbage and 2 carrots. Add a little dill and a pinch of celery seed. Mince sweet pickles. Mix some pickle juice with mayonnaise to make the mayonnaise runny and tangy. Toss everything together.

UNIVERSITY OF LOUISVILLE
# Chilled Potato Salad

*Enough for a big picnic.*

5 pounds potatoes, cooked in skins
½ cup celery, chopped
½ cup green pepper, chopped
small jar pimientos, diced (optional)
6 scallions, diced
4-5 hard-cooked eggs, diced
1 cup mayonnaise
1 teaspoon prepared mustard
4-5 tablespoons pickle liquid
8 sweet pickles, diced

Pare and dice cooked potatoes while still hot. Add other ingredients. Mix thoroughly and add more mayonnaise, if needed. Refrigerate until chilled all through. **Serves: 6-8**

.

UNIVERSITY OF DENVER
# Chef's Salad

*Easy to make.*

Chop up or sliver cooked ham, chicken, hard-cooked eggs (optional), Swiss or American cheese—a little crisp bacon tastes good, too. Mix it all up with whatever greens you have handy—spinach is fine. Add dressing and toss.

WILLIAMS COLLEGE
# Guacamole

*Like all Mexican food, this is good and easy. If avocado is the "poor man's butter" as they say in the Caribbean islands, it sure takes some of the sting out of being poor.*

2 ripe avocados, peeled
2 tablespoons onion, chopped
1 tomato, chopped
1 tablespoon lemon juice
hot sauce or chili powder to taste
salt and pepper to taste

Just mush up and serve on leafy salad greens or as a dip. **Serves: 2**

NEW YORK UNIVERSITY

# Orange-Onion Salad

1 tablespoon oil
1 tablespoon vinegar
1 teaspoon salt
¼ teaspoon pepper
¼ teaspoon sugar
1 head lettuce
2 oranges, peeled and sliced
2 onions, sliced

Mix oil, vinegar, salt, pepper, and sugar. Wash lettuce and put on plate, forming a comparatively flat surface. Arrange orange and onion slices alternately on lettuce. Pour dressing over it all just before serving.

Another way is to chop up oranges, onions, and tear lettuce into small pieces. Then toss with dressing and serve in small bowls. **Serves: 4**

UNIVERSITY OF OREGON

# Hearty Vegetable Salad

1 pound dried lentils
1 can beef broth (or use a cube)
1 cup parsley, chopped
1 cup celery, chopped
1 cup zucchini, chopped
1 cup green pepper, chopped
1 cup red pepper, chopped
1 cup onions, chopped
1 garlic clove, minced
oil and vinegar
salt and pepper to taste

Wash and pick over lentils. Drain and put in pot with water to cover. Simmer 15 minutes. Drain and put back in pot with enough beef broth to cover. If you need more liquid, add water. Add salt and pepper and bring to simmer. Cook about 40 minutes or until lentils are tender. Drain and chill. (Keep liquid to make soup in a few days.) Just before serving, mix in all the vegetables along with oil and vinegar to your taste. Serve with corn chips, pita bread, or spoon onto salad greens garnished with black olives. **Serves: 6**

HARVARD UNIVERSITY
## Hot Chef's Salad

red or green pepper
beef, cooked
chicken, cooked
onion
eggplant
brussel sprouts
cabbage, shredded
oil
tomato paste
vinegar
soy sauce
2 cheeses: 1 cubed, 1 grated
wheat germ

Cut up meat and vegetables into large chunks, except for cabbage which should be shredded. Heat oil in large skillet. The amount of oil depends on the quantity of ingredients; there should be enough to coat all the vegetables and meat. When oil is hot (but not smoking), add vegetables and stir-fry 2-3 minutes. Add beef, chicken, and tomato paste and mix thoroughly. Add vinegar, slightly less than the amount of oil used. Heat. Add soy sauce and cheese and toss to blend. Cover until cheese is melted. Sprinkle with wheat germ and serve. **Serves: Depends on quantity**

PRESCOTT COLLEGE
## Tabouli

*Very, very good—refreshing. Bulgur keeps better, both cooked and uncooked, than any other grain. Our garden is organic, so we have lots of parsley practically free. You can even grow parsley on the windowsill in a dorm.*

6 bunches parsley, chopped
3 cups cooked or soaked bulgur
2 bunches of scallions, finely chopped
3-4 tomatoes, chopped
4 tablespoons olive oil
salt to taste
¾-1 cup lemon or orange juice

Mix well, chill. Eat cold. **Serves: 4-5**

HOBART COLLEGE

# Inspiration Salad

The fun about this is that it's different every time. If you carefully save leftovers, the way we do, you end up with a couple of spoonfuls of green beans, carrots, pineapple chunks, old mushrooms, raw turnip, ham, chicken, bean sprouts, rice, hard-cooked eggs, cold potatoes, cheese, bulgur, olives, etc.

Cut up everything you want to get rid of *very, very* small. Mix with a slightly vinegary dressing. It works better if you have an oil like olive oil that has a lot of flavor. Add a minced garlic clove and some minced sweet onion. Toss until everything is thoroughly mixed with the dressing. Serve on crisp salad greens. It's delicious and everything goes together beautifully.

UNIVERSITY OF COLORADO

# Lynn's Coleslaw

*A little change from the usual coleslaw.*

¼ head cabbage, shredded
1 carrot, shredded
1 green pepper, shredded
1 small zucchini, shredded
½ cup mayonnaise
salt and pepper to taste

Mix all together. Add more mayonnaise if necessary. Very, very good on a ham or corned beef sandwich instead of lettuce. **Serves: 3-4**

UNIVERSITY OF NEW MEXICO

# Potato Salad with Yogurt

*Easy, filling, and a little different.*

6 potatoes, cooked and sliced
1 cup yogurt
1 tablespoon vinegar
½ cup raw carrots, shredded (optional)
½ cup cucumbers, chopped (optional)
salt and pepper to taste

Stir gently to combine all ingredients except potatoes. Toss potatoes gently with yogurt mixture and serve. **Serves: 2-4**

# Notes & Recipes

# SAUCES, GRAVIES, AND SALAD DRESSINGS

**Recipes included and the chief ingredients needed.**

### WINE MARINADE
Oil, soy sauce, Worcestershire sauce, mustard, wine, parsley flakes, lemon juice

### BUTTER SAUCE
Butter

### LEMON BUTTER SAUCE
Butter, lemon juice

### CURRY SAUCE (BUTTER)
Butter, curry powder or curry spices

### CLAM SAUCE (BUTTER)
Butter, chopped clams, garlic

### ONION SAUCE (BUTTER)
Butter, onions

### WHITE SAUCE
Butter, flour, milk or stock

### BROWN SAUCE OR GRAVY
Butter, flour, pan drippings or stock

### CURRY SAUCE
White or brown sauce, curry powder

### MUSHROOM SAUCE
White or brown sauce, mushrooms

### ONION SAUCE
White or brown sauce, onions

### CHEESE SAUCE
White or brown sauce, grated cheese

### FINEST SALAD DRESSING
Cider vinegar, safflower oil, paprika, basil, and other spices

### SALAD DRESSING II
Olive oil, cider or wine vinegar, garlic

### GERMAN SALAD DRESSING
Cider vinegar, sugar

### SOUR CREAM SALAD DRESSING
Sour cream, vinegar

# SAUCES, GRAVIES, AND SALAD DRESSINGS

Sauces, gravies, and salad dressings are used to add moisture and flavor to the foods they accompany. Most of them are very easy to make in spite of the fact that cookbooks often give them fancy names. They are essential if you want to make the most of leftovers, turning them into delicious meals. Sauces you make yourself save you the extra expense of canned gravies and "convenience" foods; they provide better nutrition because they do not contain the additives, "flavor enhancers,"™ and other chemicals of commercial products. Easy, inexpensive, healthier— these simple basic recipes are an indispensable part of any cook's repertoire.

VASSAR COLLEGE
# Wine Marinade

*I guess you would want to include a marinade in sauces since it's really a basting sauce you soak something in before cooking. A marinade can be reused if you have any left over. Freeze if you're not going to use it again right away.*

1½ cups peanut or other cooking oil
¾ cup soy sauce
2 teaspoons Worcestershire sauce
2 teaspoons dry mustard
1 teaspoon fresh ground pepper
1 cup dry red wine (cheap wine is acceptable)
2 teaspoons dried parsley flakes
⅓ cup fresh lemon juice (reconstituted works too)

Combine all ingredients in a quart jar. With cover on tight, shake vigorously or use blender. Marinate meat in the refrigerator for at least 3 hours—overnight is better. Turn meat at least once. **Makes: 3 ⅔ cups**

COLUMBIA UNIVERSITY
# Butter Sauces

*If a recipe calls for "drawn" or melted butter, that's a butter sauce. It's very useful.*

**Lemon Butter Sauce**: We use this for fish. It's just melted butter with salt, pepper, and lemon juice added.

**Curry Sauce**: If we don't have time to make a real curry sauce, we add curry spices (turmeric, etc.) to butter instead. Or, if you don't make your own curry, a tablespoon of ready-made curry powder to a cup of melted butter does the job.

**Clam Sauce**: Minced garlic cloves and as many chopped clams (canned are fine) as you feel like, added to melted butter, with salt and pepper is a good quick white clam sauce for spaghetti—very expensive in restaurants, very inexpensive at home.

**Onion Sauce**: Chop up onions and add them to melted butter. Brown or not, depending on the flavor you want.

We make lots of others but this should give you the idea. Lots of times we just add an herb—like tarragon for chicken, rosemary for lamb chops or for a broiled dish. **Makes: Depends on quantity**

UNIVERSITY OF PITTSBURGH

# White Sauce and Brown Sauce or Gravy

*These are the two basic sauces—very, very simple. The proportions are what is important. No matter how much or how little you want to make, always stick to these proportions (except for cheese sauce).*

2 tablespoons butter
2 tablespoons flour
1 cup of milk or stock for *white sauce* or pan
     drippings for *gravies*
seasoning to taste

Melt butter in saucepan. Blend in flour, cook 1 minute, stirring constantly. Add liquid gradually, still stirring constantly. Lower heat and cook until it thickens (a few minutes), stirring occasionally. **Makes: 1 cup**

Variations:

**Curry Sauce**: Add a tablespoon of curry powder.

**Mushroom Sauce**: Sauté sliced mushrooms in butter a few minutes before adding flour. If you want a really rich sauce, add heavy cream instead of milk.

**Onion Sauce**: Chop onions and brown in butter before adding flour and liquid.

**Cheese Sauce**: Combine 2 tablespoons butter to 1 tablespoon of flour to 1 cup milk. Then add ¾ cup grated American (or similar) cheese and heat until it blends and melts into everything else. Stir steadily all the time you are making this. It doesn't take long. Don't keep the heat too high. Cheese shouldn't be cooked at high heat.

All you have to remember is that milk or cream makes a white sauce. So does stock unless you brown the flour in a frying pan before you add it. Pan drippings make a brown sauce or gravy. After that you can add anything you want.

# Finest Salad Dressing

*My vinegar-and-oil salad dressing is the finest.*

Cider vinegar and safflower oil—slightly more vinegar than oil. Heavy dashes of turmeric, paprika, fresh ground pepper, garlic and onion powder, curry, basil, thyme, celery seed. It should look red from the paprika, heavy on the basil. Balance it out to taste.

## Salad Dressing II

But for purists, equal parts of olive oil and vinegar (cider or wine vinegar, preferably) or slightly more oil than vinegar. Minced garlic, salt, and pepper to taste. **Makes: Depends on quantity**

# German Salad Dressing

*This is also good for marinating cold vegetables, like very thinly sliced cucumbers.*

½ cup cold water
¼ cup cider vinegar
1 teaspoon salt
¼ teaspoon pepper
2 teaspoons sugar

Blend everything together and chill. It sounds simple but it's good. **Makes: ¾ cup**

# Sour Cream Salad Dressing

You can make a tart sour cream dressing by adding a couple of spoonsful of vinegar and a little salt and pepper to ½ pint of sour cream. Mix well. A variation on this is to add a tablespoon of mayonnaise as well. Or you can make a dressing that's especially good with fruit salads by adding fruit juice instead of vinegar.

# Notes & Recipes

# DESSERTS

**Recipes included and the chief ingredients needed.**

SNICKERS
Flour, butter, sugar, eggs, cream of tartar

FRUIT YOGURT
Plain yogurt, dried fruit

COLONIAL APPLE CUSTARD
Applesauce, eggs, butter

APPLESAUCE
Apples

YOGURT PIE FILLING
Pie crust, yogurt, raisins, eggs, honey

BUTTERSCOTCH BROWNIES
Brown sugar, oil, eggs, soy grits, wheat germ,
whole wheat flour, walnuts, powdered milk

GRANOLA COOKIES
Granola, flour, eggs, butter

DATE CANDY FUDGE
Sugar, dates, walnuts, milk, butter

COCONUT BLENDER PIE
Pie shell, honey, eggs, milk, flour, coconut

LEMON CHEESE PIE
Graham cracker crust, cream cheese, butter, egg,
flour, milk, lemon

APPLE CRISP
Apples, butter, flour, sugar

RICE PUDDING
Milk, honey, butter, cooked rice, eggs, raisins

CHOCOLATE CHIP TOAST
Toast, cream cheese, chocolate chips

CHOCOLATE CHIP PECAN PIE
Pie shell, eggs, cornstarch, pecans, chocolate chips

CAROB PEANUT BUTTER GOO CANDY
Carob powder, peanut butter, milk, honey

WALNUT PIE
Pie shell, eggs, corn syrup, walnuts

APPLES WITH CRÈME FRAÎCHE
Semitart apples, apple-flavored yogurt, hazelnuts

PEACH CRUNCH
Peaches, flour, wheat germ, Grape Nuts®

# DESSERTS

Dessert is something we are never too full to eat. It need be no more than a perfectly ripe peach or a wedge of melon; it may be a dish that is extra rich and gooey. If it's served with a little ceremony, like with a fruit knife and a salt shaker, it's more a company dessert than an apple grabbed from a bowl and eaten on the run. But both are satisfactory desserts and add to the pleasure of the meal that preceded them.

Most of the recipes that were sent me are easy and quick to make, and run the gamut from fruity to really rich. Several of them are like five recipes in one because they lend themselves to many variations.

TEXAS CHRISTIAN UNIVERSITY

# Snickers

*My specialty is the sweets department. As I remember it, I learned to bake in elementary school because I loved cookies and Mother, always busy with things besides baking, invariably let the bottoms of the cookies burn, then tried to get us to eat them by telling us charcoal was good for our teeth!*

**1 cup butter**
**1½ cups sugar**
**2 eggs**
**2¾ cups flour**
**2 teaspoons cream of tartar**
**1 teaspoon baking soda**
**¼ teaspoon salt**
**2 tablespoons sugar mixed with 2 tablespoons cinnamon**

Preheat oven to 400° F. Cream butter and sugar with spoon. Add eggs. Add flour, cream of tartar, baking soda, and salt mixed together. Mix thoroughly. Shape dough into 1″ balls. Roll in cinnamon sugar. Place 2″ apart on ungreased baking sheet. Bake 8-10 minutes. These cookies puff up at first and then flatten out. **Makes: 6 dozen**

BARNARD COLLEGE

# Fruit Yogurt

Mix plain or vanilla yogurt with dried fruit that has been boiled a few minutes. Keep in a jar in the icebox—much better than the too sweet, gooey fruit yogurt you buy.

If you *like* sweeter yogurt, make it yourself from plain yogurt plus a couple of spoonsful of preserves, jam, or canned fruit (with a little of the syrup). Lots cheaper and better tasting.

YALE UNIVERSITY

# Colonial Apple Custard

*This is easy to make and can be eaten as a side dish with meat or for dessert with a topping of light cream or yogurt. Makes a great pick-me-up while studying late at night.*

**1 tablespoon melted butter**
**1 cup applesauce**
**3 eggs, beaten**
**¼ teaspoon salt**

Preheat oven to 350° F. Butter 4 custard cups. Combine remaining butter, applesauce, eggs, and salt. Pour into custard cups. Bake approximately ½ hour or until knife comes out clean. May be eaten hot or cold. **Serves: 4**

UNIVERSITY OF COLORADO
# Applesauce

Peel apples. Cut up and put in pot. Cover about ¾″ high with water. Add sugar, cinnamon, clove (sparingly), nutmeg, and a little ginger—all to taste. Cook until mushy or however you like. Also very good with unpeeled apples, but don't cook them as long because all the peels fall off.

PRESCOTT COLLEGE
# Yogurt Pie Filling

*Use any recipe you like for pie crust or buy a frozen one. If you buy a frozen one, buy two and use one for the top crust.*

- 2 eggs, separated
- 1 cup yogurt
- ½-1 cup honey
- 1 cup raisins, chopped
- ½ teaspoon cinnamon
- ¼ teaspoon nutmeg
- ¼ teaspoon allspice

Preheat oven to 450° F. Beat egg yolks. Add yogurt, honey, raisins, and spices. Beat egg whites. Fold yogurt mixture into egg whites. Fill pie and top with crust. Bake for 10 minutes at 450° F. Turn oven down to 350° F and bake for 30 minutes. You can vary this by using other fruit and different sweetening. **Serves: 6**

PRESCOTT COLLEGE
# Butterscotch Brownies

- 2 cups brown sugar, packed
- ½ cup oil
- 2 large eggs, beaten
- 1 teaspoon vanilla
- ⅔ cup whole wheat flour (plus some extra for nuts and pan)
- ½ cup powdered milk
- ½ teaspoon salt
- 2 teaspoons baking powder
- ½ cup soy grits, soaked in ½ cup hot water (optional)
- ⅔ cup wheat germ
- 1 cup walnut meats

Preheat oven to 375° F. Combine sugar, oil, and eggs; mix well. Add vanilla. Add sifted flour, milk, salt, baking powder; mix. Add grits, wheat germ, walnut meats dredged in flour (so they won't sink). Bake in greased, floured pan for 25-30 minutes. Let cool 5 minutes before cutting into squares. **Serves: 6**

## Granola Cookies

1 cup sifted flour
½ teaspoon baking powder
¼ teaspoon baking soda
¼ teaspoon salt
½ cup butter, softened
1 cup dark brown sugar, packed
1 egg
1 teaspoon vanilla
2½ cups granola
¼ cup raisins (optional)

Preheat oven to 375° F. Sift together flour, baking powder, baking soda, and salt. Beat butter and sugar until light and fluffy. Add egg, vanilla; beat well. Add dry ingredients and mix well. Drop by level tablespoons onto greased baking sheet. Bake 10-12 minutes or until lightly browned. **Makes: 5 dozen approximately**

## Date Candy Fudge

3 cups sugar or whatever you use: ½ white sugar, ½ brown date sugar
1 cup fresh dates, chopped
1 cup milk (regular or ½ evaporated—the best is to use mostly evaporated milk)
1 pat of butter
1 cup walnuts, chopped

Put all together, except nuts. Bring to boil. Boil 15-20 minutes until it reaches the soft-ball stage. Take off heat. Add nuts and beat just about stiff. Pour out; let harden. Cut. **Serves: 4-6**

## Coconut Blender Pie

⅓ cup honey
4 eggs
1 cup milk
½ teaspoon salt
½ cup butter
½ cup flour
1 cup shredded coconut
1 teaspoon vanilla
1 unbaked pie shell

Preheat oven to 350° F. Put all ingredients except pie shell in blender and blend for two minutes. Pour into pie shell and bake for 30-40 minutes or until set. **Serves: 6**

PRESCOTT COLLEGE
# Lemon Cheese Pie

1 tablespoon softened butter
1 cup sugar
3 8-ounce packages cream cheese
1 egg
⅔ cup milk
¼ cup lemon juice
2 tablespoons lemon rind, grated
1 unbaked graham cracker crust

Preheat oven to 350° F. Cream butter and sugar together with spoon. Add cream cheese and egg and mix well. Add milk, lemon juice, and rind. Heat, but do not let boil. Pour hot mixture into unbaked crust made of crumbs (graham cracker, etc.) or coconut. Bake for 45 minutes. Chill thoroughly before serving. **Serves: 6**

BOSTON UNIVERSITY
# Apple Crisp

*This is easy and delishous!*

9 McIntosh apples, peeled and sliced (can substitute any type)
1 tablespoon cinnamon
½ stick butter, slightly softened
½ cup flour
½ cup sugar

Preheat oven to 350° F. Into a casserole or pan, slice the apples, sprinkling each layer generously with cinnamon. In a bowl, cream together with a spoon: butter, flour, and sugar. Spoon evenly over apples. Bake about 40 minutes. Serve warm with whipped cream. **Serves: 4-6**

UNIVERSITY OF PITTSBURGH

# Rice Pudding

*This is a great and easy dessert for us rice pudding fans.*

1⅓ cups milk
½ teaspoon salt
3½ tablespoons honey
1 tablespoon softened butter
1 teaspoon vanilla
2 eggs
2 cups rice, cooked
¼ cup raisins, previously softened in water
¼ teaspoon cinnamon

Preheat oven to 325° F. Combine and beat well: milk, salt, honey, butter, vanilla, and eggs. Add rice, raisins, and cinnamon. Grease baking dish. Pour in mixture. Sprinkle a little more cinnamon on top and bake for 1 hour. **Serves: 2**

PRESCOTT COLLEGE

# Chocolate Chip Toast

Make toast. Spread thickly with cream cheese. Sprinkle with chocolate chips.

BARNARD COLLEGE

# Chocolate Chip Pecan Pie

*This is fattening and quite decadent, but well worth the calories!*

2 eggs
1 cup sugar
½ cup melted butter
1 teaspoon vanilla
¼ cup cornstarch
1 cup pecans, finely chopped
⅔ cup chocolate chips
1 unbaked pie shell

Preheat oven to 350° F. Beat eggs lightly. Add sugar, melted butter, and vanilla. Mix well. Add enough water to cornstarch to make it a little runny. Blend cornstarch into egg mixture. Stir in pecans and chocolate chips. Spoon into unbaked pie shell. Bake for 45-50 minutes or until toothpick or knife inserted into center comes out clean. *Cool* 1 hour. Reheat and serve. **Serves: 6**

PRESCOTT COLLEGE

# Carob Peanut Butter Goo Candy

*Tastes for all the world as if it were made with chocolate. Quick to mix up when everyone feels like eating candy. No cooking!*

3 tablespoons carob powder
4 tablespoons peanut butter
2 tablespoons milk
4 tablespoons honey
chopped nuts or coconut

Mix ingredients. Beat until creamy. Refrigerate. It will stay soft but it can be sort of cut with a knife. If you freeze it, it will get a little firmer. To serve easily, shape it in small balls (about the size of large marbles) and roll in chopped nuts or coconut—not so sticky to handle. **Serves: 2**

WESLEYAN UNIVERSITY

# Walnut Pie

*I make this in my toaster oven.*

¼ cup butter
1 cup brown sugar, packed
3 eggs
½ cup light corn syrup
1-1½ cups broken walnuts
1 teaspoon vanilla
½ teaspoon salt
1 unbaked pie shell

Preheat oven to 375° F. Melt butter and add it to sugar. Stir to mix thoroughly. Beat in eggs, one at a time. Stir in corn syrup, walnuts, vanilla, and salt. Spoon into unbaked pie shell and bake 35-40 minutes. **Serves: 6**

GEORGETOWN UNIVERSITY

# Apples with Crème Fraîche

*I first discovered this while I was studying in Paris for a semester. It's quick and easy to make and really tasty. Since I haven't been able to find crème fraîche in the States, I've substituted apple-flavored yogurt.*

**semitart apples**
**apple-flavored yogurt**
**hazelnuts (finely chopped)**

The amounts to be used don't really matter. And you can use walnuts or almonds instead of hazelnuts. Pare, core, and dice the apples. Mix with yogurt and chopped nuts until the apples are well coated. Delicious as a snack, salad, or appetizer. **Serves: Depends on quantity**

UNIVERSITY OF PENNSYLVANIA

# Peach Crunch

**8-10 peaches**
**½ cup water**
**½ cup flour**
**¼ cup wheat germ**
**¼ cup Grape Nuts®**
**1 cup brown sugar, packed**
**1 teaspoon cinnamon**
**½ cup butter**

Preheat oven to 350° F. Peel and slice peaches and put in deep dish pie pan or medium-sized casserole. Pour water over peaches. Combine cinnamon and ½ cup sugar and sprinkle over peaches. Combine flour, butter, and remaining sugar and mix with a fork, mashing butter into flour and sugar until there are no large pieces of butter and texture is crumbly. Add wheat germ and Grape Nuts® and mix well. Spread over peaches, pressing down firmly. Bake 30 minutes until peaches are soft and top is browned. Serve with whipped cream or plain yogurt. **Serves: 4-6**

# Notes & Recipes

# THINGS TO EAT WHEN YOU HAVE TO STAY UP ALL NIGHT STUDYING

**Recipes included and the chief ingredients needed.**

HAM AND APPLE CASSEROLE
Ham, apples, onions, milk

JODI'S BANANA SHAKE
Bananas, milk, honey

EGGY HAM TOAST
Ham, cream, egg yolk, toast

BAKED BEAN RAREBIT
Baked beans, American cheese, milk, egg, toast

SUN-BREWED TEA
Tea, water, sun

ANN'S MIDNIGHT SNACK SPECIALTY
Potatoes, onion, garlic

MIKE'S THREE-BEAN CASSEROLE
Kidney, soy and pinto beans, tomato paste, chili powder

JOCKO'S OVEN DELIGHT
Onions, tomatoes, sharp cheese, bread crumbs

WELSH RABBIT
Flour, milk, cheese, toast

JERRY'S DAD'S BABY PIZZA
English muffins, tomato sauce, pepperoni, green pepper, onions, mushrooms

COLD DORM DRINK
Orange juice, Jello®

DENISE'S TORTILLA CHIP SALAD
Lettuce, ground beef, kidney beans, tomatoes, tortilla chips, cheddar cheese, onion, mayonnaise, chili sauce, pickle relish

SMOOTHIES
Bananas, honey, fruit

WAFFLES
Eggs, flour, sugar, milk

# THINGS TO EAT WHEN YOU HAVE TO STAY UP ALL NIGHT STUDYING

WILLIAM SMITH COLLEGE

## Eggy Ham Toast

2 cups cream
1 egg yolk
1 cup boiled or baked ham, finely chopped
salt and pepper to taste

Scald cream. Beat yolk and add to cream. Stir until mixture thickens. Add chopped ham and cook only until it is hot—very soon. Serve on toast. **Serves: 2**

GODDARD COLLEGE
# Jodi's Banana Shake

*A good pick-up when you need one.*

2 cups milk
2 bananas, sliced
1 tablespoon honey
dash of cinnamon
almost 1 teaspoon vanilla

Put all ingredients in blender. Then add 1 or 2 ice cubes. Blend until ice is chopped or instead of ice, add two scoops of ice cream—chocolate is good. **Serves: 1**

UNIVERSITY OF DENVER
# Sun-brewed Tea

*One way to have good tea inexpensively is to let the sun brew it.*

Get a gallon jug. Fill with water—spring water preferably. Add 3 tablespoons of tea or 3 teabags early in the morning. Put it outside somewhere where it will get the sun all day. It will brew with a unique flavor—the water is kinder because it doesn't bruise the leaves the way boiling water does. Very refreshing.

UNION COLLEGE, SCHENECTADY, NY
# Baked Bean Rarebit

2 tablespoons butter
1 cup American cheese, grated
1 cup milk
salt and pepper to taste
¼ teaspoon dry mustard
1 cup baked beans, mashed
1 egg, slightly beaten

Melt butter in pan, stir in cheese, milk, and seasonings gradually until mixture is perfectly smooth. Add beans and egg. Stir and cook until hot (very soon). Serve over toast. **Serves: 2**

UNIVERSITY OF TEXAS
# Ham and Apple Casserole

*Someone makes this in the afternoon so it is all ready to put in the oven an hour before we think we are going to want it.*

Equal amount of ham, tart apples, and onions. The ham should be cooked. Slice into buttered casserole in layers, starting with apples. Dot each layer with butter and sprinkle with salt and pepper. Repeat until you have as much as you need to feed whoever will be eating. Pour in milk about ⅔ up the casserole. Top with buttered bread crumbs. An hour before you want to eat, put it in a 400° F oven and bake covered for 45 minutes, uncovered for 15 minutes.

HUMBOLDT STATE UNIVERSITY

# Ann's Midnight Snack Specialty

*Better than french fries!*

3 potatoes, sliced and cooked
1 onion, coarsely chopped
1 garlic clove, minced
butter
salt to taste

Sauté onion and garlic in butter until onion is translucent. Add potatoes and any other seasonings you're in the mood for. Toss to blend and cook until potatoes are heated through and as crisp and browned as you want them. Serve hot. **Serves: 2**

MASSACHUSETTS INSTITUTE OF TECHNOLOGY

# Mike's Three-Bean Casserole

⅓ cup each cooked kidney, soy, and pinto
     beans (or any other combination you like)
½ can tomato paste
salt, pepper, and chili powder to taste

Combine in pot with water to cover, stirring to combine with paste. Simmer on top of stove (or in oven, if you prefer) until hot and well blended. The mixture will get thicker the longer it cooks; it starts out soupy and ends up a stew if you keep cooking. Quantities are not crucial—you can use more or less tomato paste, lots of chili powder, more water, etc. **Serves: 1**

TEXAS CHRISTIAN UNIVERSITY

# Jocko's Oven Delight

*This is best made in a round ovenware casserole, 1- or 2-quart size, depending on number of eaters.*

*To make 1 quart*:
3 large onions
4 tomatoes
1 pound sharp cheese
1 cup buttered bread crumbs

Slice all ingredients thinly. If you don't have a tomato knife, your knife will have to be very sharp to do this ·successfully. Salt and pepper vegetables. Layer onions, then cheese, and then tomatoes in casserole until almost full. Bake on middle rack of oven for about 1 hour. Top with bread crumbs and continue baking until crumbs are golden brown. If doubling all quantities, use 2-quart casserole. **Serves: 3-4**

COLUMBIA UNIVERSITY

# Welsh Rabbit

Melt 1 tablespoon butter in pan. Add 1 tablespoon flour, mix well. Add ½ cup milk, cook until thick. Add 1 handful of grated cheese—cheddar or any leftover cooking cheese you have. Stir until melted and blended. Add a little dry mustard. Serve over toast. Just enough for 1 person.

UNIVERSITY OF COLORADO

# Jerry's Dad's Baby Pizza

Cut English muffins in half. Place in flat pan. Spread tomato sauce on each half. For each half muffin, place 3 slices of pepperoni over tomato sauce. Add slices of green pepper rings, onion rings, sliced mushrooms. Top with slices of mozzarella cheese. Bake in 350° F oven until toasty and melted. We usually figure 4 halves apiece but we eat large portions.

UNIVERSITY OF DENVER

# Cold Dorm Drink

*This is a good drink for dorm residents who have no cooking facilities.*

Take an empty jar with a tight-fitting lid. Put in 1 part orange juice, one part powdered Jello® (I like raspberry). Add cold water from the water fountain. Put on lid and shake it up. Better than a Coke®.

UNIVERSITY OF TEXAS

# Denise's Tortilla Chip Salad

1 head lettuce
1 pound ground beef
¾ teaspoon seasoned salt
½ teaspoon each: onion powder, garlic
    powder, chili powder
⅛ teaspoon cayenne pepper
4 drops red pepper sauce
⅔ cup water
1 14-ounce can kidney beans, drained
4 tomatoes, cut into eighths
1 6¼-ounce package tortilla chips
1 cup cheddar cheese (about 4 ounces),
    shredded
1 cup onion, chopped
½ cup mayonnaise or salad dressing
¼ cup chili sauce
1 tablespoon pickle relish

Wash lettuce and shred. Chill at least 1 hour. Brown ground beef in large skillet. Drain fat. Stir in seasonings, water, and kidney beans. Simmer, uncovered for 15 minutes, stirring occasionally. Cool 10 minutes. Combine greens, tomatoes, tortilla chips, onions and cheese in large salad bowl. Mix together mayonnaise, chili sauce, and pickle relish. Toss gently with salad mixture. Pour warm ground beef mixture over salad. Toss gently. *Serve immediately.* **Serves: 4-6**

UNIVERSITY OF DENVER

# Smoothies

*I got this from some students at the University of California in Santa Barbara. They have a small permanent booth where they sell just this drink—usually 10 different kinds on the menu any given day.*

bananas
fruit (any kind except dried apples, I
    recommend strawberries)
honey
water

Peel bananas and cut in 3 sections. Freeze. Will keep indefinitely if necessary. Remove from freezer. Put in blender, add fruit, 1 or 2 teaspoons honey, and enough water so blender will operate. Turn on blender. When liquid is smooth, it is ready to drink.

Vary it any way you can think of. Try a little orange juice (it will make it thinner), cinnamon, or nutmeg. If you use fruits that don't have as strong a taste as bananas, you may need to use more of those fruits. **Serves: Depends on quantity**

BOSTON COLLEGE

# Waffles

*When exams start, we make this in large quantities and refrigerate it; then anyone who gets hungry at odd hours can quickly make waffles. We got a used waffle iron for practically nothing at Goodwill.*

3 eggs, beaten
2 cups flour (best if 1 cup is whole wheat
    flour)
2 tablespoons baking soda
1 tablespoon sugar
1 teaspoon vanilla
4 tablespoons melted butter
approximately 1 ¼ cups milk (add gradually
    until batter is a good consistency for
    pouring onto waffle iron)

Mix ingredients. Just before cooking, add 1 cup of mashed bananas or 1 cup of blueberries for extra nutrition. **Serves: 4**

# FOOD FOR FRIENDS AND OTHER GUESTS

**Recipes included and the chief ingredients needed.**

### NANCY'S MEXICAN RICE
Rice, jalapeño peppers, tomatoes

### HOT POTATO SALAD
Potatoes

### HUNGARIAN GOULASH
Sauerkraut, white wine, stew beef, onions, tomatoes, caraway seeds, sour cream

### NANCY'S ENCHILADAS
Tortillas, ground beef, pinto beans, onion, Monterey Jack, cheddar cheese, enchilada sauce

### FABULOUS FROZEN PIZZA
Frozen pizza, oregano, basil, Parmesan cheese, mushrooms, mozzarella cheese, green/red pepper

### SAUTÉED CABBAGE
Cabbage, cream, caraway seeds

### PAT'S PIZZA
Yeast, mozzarella cheese, pepperoni or sausage, pizza sauce

### STEVE'S PAELLA
Chicken, mussels, onions, canned tomatoes, garlic, green peppers, shrimp, sausage, peas, pimientos

### BAKED PORK CHOPS WITH HERBS
Pork chops, bread crumbs, thyme, parsley, chives

### LULI KEBAB
Ground meat, onions, fresh parsley, lemons, dill

### CRANBERRY RIBS
Spareribs, onions, honey, chili sauce, ketchup, garlic, whole cranberry sauce, cloves, orange juice, grated orange rind

### FRENCH-FRIED ONION RINGS
Onion, flour, egg, milk, baking powder

### INDIAN RICE
Rice, cooked chicken, chicken broth, peanuts, raisins, curry powder, turmeric, ginger

### CARAMEL POPCORN
Popcorn, brown sugar, corn syrup, baking soda, vanilla

### CHILI AND CHEESE CASSEROLE
Spinach, cottage cheese, eggs, onion, garlic, caraway seeds, herbs, grated cheese

### CHOW MEIN
Oil, onion, mushrooms, bean sprouts, water chestnuts, chicken, ginger, chicken broth, soy sauce, cornstarch

# FOOD FOR FRIENDS AND OTHER GUESTS

## MIDDLEBURY COLLEGE

## Nancy's Mexican Rice

Make rice as usual and mix with 1 can jalapeño peppers and tomatoes. The tomatoes can be fresh and coarsely chopped or canned and well drained. Proportions will vary according to how well seasoned and how moist you want the rice to be.

    **Serving suggestion**: Add a cup of nuts, finely chopped, mix well with the rice, and serve with a tossed salad for an inexpensive supper.

JOHNS HOPKINS UNIVERSITY

# Hot Potato Salad

*Quick, good, and filling. Goes with everything from hamburgers to bologna. If you want to make a lot, just double everything.*

**6 potatoes**
**¼ cup cider vinegar**
**3 tablespoons hot water**
**3 tablespoons sugar**
**salt and pepper to taste**

Boil potatoes in their skins until easily pierced with a fork. Small potatoes take about 20-25 minutes; larger ones take longer. Don't start poking them too soon or you will break them up. Drain. Cool until you can handle them. Peel and slice, but work quickly so they will stay as warm as possible. Combine all other ingredients in small sauce pan and heat to boiling. Pour over potatoes and toss for a minute over very low heat to get them hot again. Do this very gently or you will have hot diced potatoes. This is good cold the next day if any is left over. **Serves: 2-4**

DUKE UNIVERSITY

# Hungarian Goulash

*My friends thought I was kidding when I said I was making this, but not after they tasted it.*

**2 large cans sauerkraut**
**1 cup white wine (optional)**
**4 pounds stewing beef, cubed**
**3 tablespoons peanut oil**
**4 cups onions, thinly sliced**
**2 cups canned tomatoes, chopped**
**4 tablespoons paprika**
**1 tablespoon caraway seeds**
**salt to taste**
**3 cups sour cream**

Pour wine over sauerkraut, mix, and put aside. Heat oil in heavy pot or skillet and brown beef on all sides. Add all other ingredients except sour cream. If too dry, add 1 cup of water. It may be necessary to add more later as it cooks. Check every so often to make sure there is enough liquid for cooking and serving. Simmer, covered, about 1 hour, or until meat is tender. It is better to overcook than to serve tough meat. Take off the heat and stir in sour cream. Cover and let stand to reheat. (If you put the pot back on the heat and the liquid boils, your sour cream may curdle.) **Serves: 8-10**

 **Serving idea**: Traditional over egg noodles, but rice works fine if that is handier.

MIDDLEBURY COLLEGE
# Nancy's Enchiladas

*These, plus* Nancy's Mexican Rice *(see page 143), will serve 4-6 people. If your budget won't stand for that, add more beans in proportion to the meat. The recipe is very forgiving and you can use very little beef and lots more beans, onions, and cheese, if you like. Since the number of people served is limited by the number of tortillas you fill, plan accordingly.*

12 tortillas (frozen are cheapest)
2-3 tablespoons peanut oil
1 pound ground beef
1 8-ounce can pinto beans
1 medium onion, diced
Monterey Jack and mild cheddar cheese, diced

Sauce:
1-2 cans hot or mild enchilada sauce *or* 8 teaspoons chili powder plus 1 small can tomatoes
2 tablespoons flour
1½ cups water (omit if you use tomatoes)
garlic powder to taste

Preheat oven to 350° F. Brown meat. Drain fat and add beans. Cook until hot. Heat about ¼" oil in frying pan and fry each tortilla for a few seconds on each side, but don't allow to get crisp. Place in baking dish, fill with 1-2 spoonsful bean mixture, some onions, and some cheese, then roll. Prepare all tortillas the same way. Cover with sauce and sprinkle top with cheese. Bake until cheese melts completely and is bubbly. To feed more, serve with refried beans as well as *Mexican Rice.* **Serves: 4-6**

WESLEYAN
# Fabulous Frozen Pizza

*This is the only way to eat frozen pizza!*

frozen pizza

Preheat oven as indicated on box. Choose any of the better brands of frozen pizza. Take from box and sprinkle frozen pizza with 2-4 tablespoons olive oil. Top with oregano, sweet basil, Parmesan cheese (grated), canned or sautéed sliced mushrooms, grated mozzarella cheese, green and/or red pepper, and some paprika. Cook as directed.

SYRACUSE UNIVERSITY

# Sautéed Cabbage

*Serve this with Sweet-Sour Meatballs (page 58) for a super party. (You'll have to double the meatball recipe.)*

1 small head cabbage
2 tablespoons oil
½ cup cream
½ teaspoon dry mustard
3 tablespoons vinegar
¼ cup caraway seeds
salt and pepper to taste

Shred cabbage. Heat oil in large skillet and add cabbage, tossing to coat with oil. Combine vinegar, mustard, caraway seeds, salt, and pepper. Continue tossing cabbage for about 8 minutes, then add vinegar mixture. Toss to blend and heat through. Remove from heat and add cream, tossing to blend. Cover, let stand a few minutes, then serve. **Serves: 4**

UNIVERSITY OF CONNECTICUT

# Pat's Pizza

*Pizzas have become so expensive that we make our own. From start to table this takes approximately 1 hour and 20 minutes—time to wash bowls and listen to some music.*

3 cups flour
1 cup warm water
1 package yeast
1 teaspoon sugar
2 tablespoons oil
8-10 ounces mozzarella cheese
½ pound ground round or pepperoni or sausage
10 ounces pizza sauce or make your own

Grease bowl. Mix flour, yeast, and sugar in bowl. Add water, mixing with greased spoon until evenly moist. Add oil gradually. Knead dough on board for 5 minutes. Put back in bowl. Cover and let rise in warm, moist area until double in bulk—takes about 1 hour. While dough is rising, grate cheese, shred meat if necessary. To make your own pizza sauce, simmer together tomato paste, olive oil, oregano, garlic salt, salt, and pepper.

While dough is rising, all utensils can be cleaned and put away. The baker is left with dough bowl, cheese bowl, and sauce bowl only.

Preheat oven to 400° F. Spread dough evenly and flat on greased cookie sheet. Add topping, sauce, and cheese, in that order. Bake on second rack from the top until cheese browns, about 15-20 minutes. **Serves: 4**

CORNELL UNIVERSITY
## Steve's Paella

*The main ingredients can be changed according to what is cheapest at the time. Pork can be substituted for chicken, clams for mussels, some white fish for shrimp. You can use all meat or all fish, and so forth. The seasoning and rice should stay the same.*

1 frying chicken, cut up
4-5 dozen mussels, scrubbed and debearded
2 onions, minced
1 large can tomatoes
3 garlic cloves, minced
2 green peppers, cut in strips
1 pound shrimp
¾ cup olive oil
3 pounds mild sausage
2 cups peas
a pinch of saffron or enough turmeric to color rice
5 cups rice
5 pimientos, sliced in strips
salt to taste

In a really large skillet (or paella pan if you have one) fry chicken and sausages until brown. Add tomatoes, garlic, and green pepper and simmer 10 minutes. Add all other ingredients, except shellfish, and 10 cups of hot water. Stir to mix thoroughly. Cook, covered, until rice is almost done, about 20 minutes. Add shellfish, laying them on top of mixture. Cook until shrimp turn pink and mussels open, about 10 minutes. (Be sure to discard any mussels that don't open.) **Serves: 8-10**

UNIVERSITY OF VIRGINIA
## Baked Pork Chops with Herbs

*Serve this recipe with baked sweet potatoes and vegetables topped with a pat of butter and sealed in foil and you have a delicious meal—all made at the same time and no work.*

8 pork chops, not too thick
4 cups bread crumbs, freshly made or purchased
½ cup peanut or safflower oil
3 tablespoons thyme
1 cup parsley, minced
4 tablespoons garlic salt
1½ cups chives, chopped
salt and pepper to taste

Preheat oven to 400° F. Trim excess fat from chops. Combine all other ingredients and mix thoroughly. One by one, press pork chops down on bread-crumb mix, coating both sides of chop. Lay chops in a single layer on foil-covered pan. If any bread crumbs are left when you finish, add them to the top of the pork chops, pressing the mixture onto the top of the chops. Bake for 1 hour. **Serves: 4-8**

# Luli Kebab

*Skewered hamburger is different and makes a great party with salad and French bread.*

3 pounds ground meat
3 onions, minced
1 cup fresh parsley, minced
2 tablespoons grated lemon rind
1 tablespoon paprika
1 tablespoon garlic salt
2 tablespoons dill, minced (optional)
½ cup lemon juice

Combine all ingredients, except lemon juice, in a bowl. Mix thoroughly with your hands. Roll into small balls and thread on bamboo skewers. (You can buy them cheaply in bundles of 100.) Shape each ball around the skewer so it looks more like a hot dog than a ball. Put on as many as the skewer will hold, but keep them all the same thickness so they will cook evenly. Pour lemon juice over the skewered meat. Arrange on a rack in a broiler pan and broil. When serving, pour the pan juices over the meat, unless the hamburger is too fat. In that case, serve without gravy but with a bowl of plain yogurt. **Serves: 6-8**

# Cranberry Ribs

2 pounds spareribs
½ cup onions, chopped
½ cup honey
½ cup chili sauce
½ cup ketchup
1 garlic clove, minced
¼ teaspoon ground cloves
1 can whole cranberry sauce
3 tablespoons vinegar
¼ cup orange juice
1 teaspoon grated orange rind
1 teaspoon salt

Preheat oven to 350° F. Combine all ingredients except spareribs in a saucepan. Heat until simmering, stirring to blend. Meanwhile, line a pan large enough to lay all the ribs flat in one layer (you may have to cut them into a couple of pieces) with enough aluminum foil to be able to bring over the top of the pan to cover it. Pour cranberry mixture over ribs. Cover with foil and bake 1 ½ hours, basting occasionally. (When you open the foil to baste, be careful of the steam.) Uncover, baste again and bake 20 minutes or until nicely browned. **Serves: 4**

## HUMBOLDT STATE UNIVERSITY

# French-fried Onion Rings

1 onion, sliced and separated into rings
1 cup flour
1 egg
1 cup milk
1 teaspoon baking powder
1½ teaspoons salt

Combine all ingredients except onion rings and beat until smooth. Let stand 15 minutes. Dip onion rings in batter and deep fry until golden brown and crisp. If you aren't serving them right away, drain on paper towels and keep warm in 300° F oven. **Serves: 1**

## NORTHWESTERN UNIVERSITY

# Indian Rice

2 cups rice, uncooked
3 cups cooked chicken, shredded
5 cups chicken broth
2 cups peanuts, chopped
1½ cups raisins
1 tablespoon curry powder
2 teaspoons turmeric
1 tablespoon ginger
salt to taste

Combine all ingredients in heavy skillet. Cover and simmer until liquid is absorbed and rice is tender. Takes about 30 minutes. Do not lift cover until the half hour is up. **Serves: 4-6**

## CORNELL UNIVERSITY

# Caramel Popcorn

8 quarts popcorn, popped
2 cups light brown sugar, packed
½ cup light corn syrup
½ pound butter
½ teaspoon baking soda
1 teaspoon vanilla

Preheat oven to 250° F. Measure popcorn into large pan. Combine sugar, syrup, and butter in separate pan and boil 5 minutes, stirring to combine. Add soda and vanilla and stir to blend. Pour over popcorn and mix until all the kernels are coated. Bake until dry, about 1 hour and 15 minutes, stirring every 15 minutes. When stirring be sure to lift off bottom pan—you may want to use a spatula for this part. **Serves: 6-8**

HUMBOLDT STATE UNIVERSITY

# Chili and Cheese Casserole

2 packages chopped spinach, cooked and
  drained
2 cups creamed cottage cheese
4 eggs, beaten
1 onion, chopped
1 garlic clove, minced
2 tablespoons butter
2 teaspoons caraway seeds
2 teaspoons seasoned salt (optional)
1 teaspoon pepper
2 tablespoons chili powder
2 pinches thyme and/or rosemary
grated cheese

Preheat oven to 350° F. Mix spinach and cottage cheese. Stir in eggs. Sauté onions in butter, adding chili powder, caraway seeds, and seasonings until onions turn translucent. Combine with eggs and put in casserole. Sprinkle with grated cheese. Bake about 25 minutes or until eggs are set. Be careful about the spinach; you will need to press it with a spoon to get the liquid out or it will make the casserole watery. **Serves: 4**

STANFORD UNIVERSITY

# Chow Mein

2 tablespoons oil (peanut or peanut and
  sesame mixed)
1 celery stalk, chopped
1 small onion, cut into large chunks
1 6-ounce can mushrooms, drained
1 cup bean sprouts
1 can water chestnuts, drained and sliced
1 cup cooked chicken, diced
2 teaspoons grated fresh ginger
½ cup chicken broth
2 tablespoons soy sauce
1 tablespoon cornstarch
chow mein noodles and rice

Heat oil in large frying pan. Stir-fry celery and onion for 3 minutes. Turn heat to low and add mushrooms, bean sprouts, water chestnuts, chicken, ginger, and chicken broth. Cover and cook for 10 minutes or until vegetables are hot all through but still crisp. Blend cornstarch with soy sauce and stir into chow mein mixture, cooking until sauce thickens (very fast). Place portion of chow mein noodles on each plate. Place rice on top of noodles. Spoon over with chow mein. **Serves: 2**

# INDEX